broken land

POEMS OF BROOKLYN

broken land

POEMS OF BROOKLYN

EDITED BY
Julia Spicher Kasdorf
& Michael Tyrell

FOREWORD BY
Hal Sirowitz

*Published in association with
the Center for American Places*

NEW YORK UNIVERSITY PRESS
NEW YORK AND LONDON

NEW YORK UNIVERSITY PRESS
New York and London
www.nyupress.org

Library of Congress Cataloging-in-Publication Data
Broken land : poems of Brooklyn / edited by Julia Kasdorf and Michael Tyrell.
p. cm.
"Published in association with the Center for American Places."
Features 125 poems about Brooklyn, by 115 poets, spanning the 17th century
to modern day. Arranged chronologically.
Includes index.
ISBN-13: 978-0-8147-4802-2 (cloth : alk. paper)
ISBN-10: 0-8147-4802-3 (cloth : alk. paper)
ISBN-13: 978-0-8147-4803-9 (pbk. : alk. paper)
ISBN-10: 0-8147-4803-1 (pbk. : alk. paper)

1. Brooklyn (New York, N.Y.)—Poetry.
2. American poetry—New York (State)—New York.
I. Kasdorf, Julia, 1962-
II. Tyrell, Michael.
PS549.N5B85   2007
811.008'03274723—dc22   2006030540

New York University Press books are printed on acid-free paper,
and their binding materials are chosen for strength and durability.

Manufactured in the United States of America
c 10 9 8 7 6 5 4 3 2 1
p. 10 9 8 7 6 5 4 3 2 1

In memory of Enid Dame

[1943–2003]

contents

foreword

Hal Sirowitz

When my parents took me to Coney Island, Brooklyn, to ride the amusements and eat at Nathan's Famous Hot Dogs, I could tell from the first bite that Paradise was slightly overcooked. "That's what happens," father said, "When companies go national. Nathan's should have just stayed in Brooklyn." But if a whole baseball team could be packed and shipped to Los Angeles, then hot dogs would be next. As soon as a frankfurter is eaten away from the beach, it doesn't taste the same. It becomes flavorless, like other brands.

This anthology doesn't have that problem. It travels well. It's so full of the sights and sounds of Brooklyn streets, that it's the next best thing to being there. Whether reading it makes you nostalgic or compels you to take the next subway to experience it for the first time, this collection maps the human heart's desire to live in a utopian community. And even though most of the utopian aspects of Brooklyn are gone, it's invigorating to still see traces: for example, the largest private food co-op in the United States, Frederick Olmstead's Prospect Park, landscaped after Central Park so he could correct his mistakes. This book isn't only for Brooklyn residents but for all those who value community. It may take the world to make a village, but it must have taken the editors many trips to different libraries to find these poems.

The former Brooklyn Poet Laureate, D. Nurkse, said, "Brooklyn is a place where you can tell the residents have *lived* lives." And editors Kasdorf and Tyrell have collected *lived* poems. Like the book title, *A Tree Grows in Brooklyn*, poetry is also endemic to this borough. Reading this collection is a moving experience because the poems feel home-grown. It doesn't matter where they were written, each one makes Brooklyn come alive, and the poems find a home inside you.

My father always joked about the guy who was stupid enough to buy the Brooklyn Bridge. That's probably an urban legend. But after reading *Broken Land*, you understand what makes it seem true and why the guy was tempted. Who wouldn't like to own an entrance way into the borough which is as exciting and less disappointing than the place Dorothy was searching for? Wizards in Brooklyn only hide their faces on Halloween. The authors of these poems never tried to buy the bridge, but they did buy into the dream of Brooklyn. Judging from the mastery and enduring quality of their poems, it was well worth it.

I was the Poet Laureate of Queens from the years 2001 to 2003. Before my term officially expired, I had already moved to Park Slope, Brooklyn. I felt like a traitor. I couldn't stop fighting the urge to come to Brooklyn. I finally left Flushing, thinking Brooklyn would become my next stepping stone to Manhattan. But once I got here, I knew I'd stay. It also helped that my wife lived here. Living in the same place is good for a marriage.

Even though Frank Sinatra sang that if you can make it in Manhattan you can make it anywhere, I'd rather make it in Brooklyn. Manhattan didn't have as strong a pull. I've grown immune to its gravity. It's true Brooklyn's big cultural institution, BAM, the Brooklyn Academy of Music, sounds like the explosion of a cannon. And another major art community, DUMBO, is also the name of an elephant in a Walt Disney film. A performing stage is called Galapagos, which are a group of islands on another continent. But that doesn't stop artists and their fans from coming here. And you'll probably be counted as one of them after reading this book, because to know Brooklyn is to love her. And love gets stronger the closer you are.

Hal Sirowitz is the author of *Mother Said*.

Introduction

Bridge, Subway, Carnival
The Poetry of Brooklyn

I. In Brooklyn, In Paradise
Michael Tyrell
and Julia Spicher Kasdorf

> Poor thing.
> To die and never see Brooklyn.
> —Anne Sexton, "Rumplestiltskin"

You furnish your parts toward eternity, / *Great or small, you furnish your parts toward the soul.* With "Sun-down Poem" (better known by its later title, "Crossing Brooklyn Ferry"), Whitman ushers in the idea of Brooklyn as a passageway both nautical and spiritual, a route that makes time irrelevant, an artificial construct. Prior to its 1898 incorporation as one of New York City's five boroughs, Brooklyn was an independent city of great size, but Whitman's is the first famous poetic example we have of Brooklyn celebrated in such a grand style, with its distinctness and uniqueness intact, "its beautiful hills" encouraged to stand up beside the "tall masts of Mannahatta." Does he contradict himself? Of course he does; he contains multitudes. When, in the same poem, Whitman insists that "place avails not," he can't help himself from claiming Brooklyn as his own. It's a claim many poets have not been able to resist since.

But long before the place found its way into modern American poetry, it—and all of the earth—was celebrated by the Lenape in a creation myth included here through what is said to be a translation from the nineteenth century. The land that would eventually be called Brooklyn was part of the vast trade network used by various branches of the Canarsies, who were eventually decimated by disease and driven farther east into Long Island, or west to what is now New Jersey. Although "Canarsie" meant "grassy place" or "fenced-in place," these tribes were known for importing and exporting. (During the construction of the Brooklyn Bridge, an immense ancient gorget was excavated, which must have been carried half a continent by foot and boat from copper mines near Lake Superior.) Only traces of the Canarsie communities still remain, and only visionary historians can see them: the great Lenape transportation "hub" that existed one block from what is now the Long Island Rail Road terminal; the old trail that is now Kings Highway; or the grass plants that resemble maize still growing on the Belt Parkway near Bay Ridge, where a vast cornfield once stood. In 1635, Dutch colonists laid out the plans for the group of villages they would call Breukelen, which was later anglicized to Brookland and eventually became Brooklyn. Tradition has long asserted that "Brooklyn" is simply the Dutch term for "broken land," but actually *gebroken landt* (broken land) is a Dutch translation of the Algonquin name for Long Island. The Dutch West India Company chartered The Town of Breukelen in 1646. (A year before, the English had chartered the Town of Gravesend, the only non-Dutch town of the six originals.) The Towns of Flatbush, Flatlands, New Utrecht, and Bushwick followed; they would be joined as Kings County in 1683. The Town of Brooklyn would have to wait until 1834 to become the City of Brooklyn, and then, in 1898, the Borough of Brooklyn. To many, it was a city overshadowed by its larger sister, Manhattan.

If "Crossing Brooklyn Ferry" considers the space between Brooklyn and Manhattan, and the idea that these as well as all places and times are intimately connected yet still worlds apart, then Hart Crane's "Bridge" gives us a more condensed but no less complex meditation. His famous "Proem" attributes to John Augustus Roebling's creation—which was still in the future when Whitman rode his ferry—a power "to lend a myth to God." Crane's is a myth working in reverse, a divine belief or explanation arrived at not because a natural phenomenon needs to be understood but because it is a manmade phenomenon that points to the idea of the divine. Even in the dreary quotidian routine summarized first by the seagull's flight and later the pedestrian's travels across the bridge, Brooklyn emerges as the gateway to America, even to the earth itself. This is no Eden but a mechanical, roughly fashioned haven, a place where paradise is hard-won, invented, Promethean.

Vladimir Mayakovsky, Russia's most famous Futurist poet, visited the bridge during the 1920s and extravagantly praised its cables "strung up / to the feet of stars," through which Manhattan's light appears almost homey in the dusk, the rumble of an elevated train reduced to a distant itch. Staggered by the inequities of "the un-united states / of / America," where radio and air travel are within reach of some while others jump from the bridge in desperate want of work, his poem, newly translated for this collection, identifies its own creation with the construction of the bridge—gestures as aesthetic as they are heroic.

The majestic and improbable Brooklyn Bridge, completed in 1883, cost Roebling his life but survives as a monument to his enterprising spirit—not the least of its reasons for becoming such a pervasive presence in American poetry. If we take to heart the British poet Geoffrey Godbert's odd and appealing found poem and collage, which gathers fragments of Roebling's writings to yield a definition of the bridge, then we may say that the builder possessed some insight into his creation's power to inspire. Starting with the technical language of bridge building, its "catenary curve[s]" and "perfect bi-system[s]," Godbert concludes with a dizzying series of constructions: " 'a Hanging Garden, a Pyramid, / an Acropolis, an Atheneaum, / a Bridge.' " There must be tributes that celebrate the Statue of Liberty, the Seattle Needle, the John Hancock Building, but we doubt so many, so varied. An entire anthology of Brooklyn Bridge poems might be possible, and perhaps in the spirit of such poetic significance, every summer the organization Poets House holds a walk across the bridge. At the culmination of the occasion, when the thing has been crossed, the walkers are revived by a public reading of "Crossing Brooklyn Ferry." It is a rich fulfillment of Whitman's prophecy that "[o]thers will enter the gates of ferry and cross from shore."

A century after Whitman, Marianne Moore's 1960 essay "Brooklyn from Clinton Hill" reminds us that Brooklyn is a "city of trees" as well as a city of churches. More than one species of tree grows in Brooklyn, as visitors to the Brooklyn Botanic Garden well know. By "trees," Moore could also mean not only arboreal specimens but rich cultural and educational institutions such as the Brooklyn Museum, Erasmus Hall, or even the botanical garden itself, whose cornucopia of plant species has attracted botanists and Brooklynites alike since its 1910 founding. Moore's rapacious view leads us on a tour of nearly every neighborhood, emphasizing the particularity of each. A resident of Brooklyn from 1929 until the late 1960s, Moore wrote of the bridge also, in "Granite and Steel," but we thought her encouragement of the Brooklyn Dodgers (1890–1957) would speak best for her here. The team relocated a coast away, but in "Hometown Piece for Messrs. Alston and Reese," Moore's characteristic fascination with athletes meets her affection for her adopted city. "Brooklyn from Clinton Hill" ends memorably: "I like living here. Brooklyn has given me pleasure, has helped to educate me, has afforded me, in fact, the kind of tame excitement on which I thrive." In another piece that touches upon education, the contemporary poet Jeffrey Harrison finds, in his "Garbage Can in Brooklyn Full of Books," titles by Adler, Hanh, Mill, and Schweitzer—a counterpoint to the borough's lowbrow reputation. And it's no tame excitement that spurs Moore to write to the Dodgers:

> You've got plenty: Jackie Robinson
> and Campy and big Newk, and Dodgerdom again
> watching everything you do. You won last year. Come on.

Because there's more to a bridge than its cables and more to a city than its skyline and baseball teams (as New York's stalwart response to the tragedy of September 11 has demonstrated), many other Brooklyn lives and Brooklyn worlds come alive in the poems written since Whitman and Crane, Moore and Bishop. Each could be said to stand as an invitation to enter a place ingeniously diverse in its cultures and neighborhoods. Broken land, we may say, eclectic palimpsest, a place for which Yeats's lines from "Crazy Jane Talks with the Bishop" might have been written: "For nothing can be sole or whole / That has not been rent." Birthplace to Mae West, Edward G. Robinson, Woody Allen, Barbra

Streisand, Bobby Fischer, Lil' Kim; Coney Island; Dreamland;
Luna Park; Ebbets Field, the one-time home of the Dodgers
(originally called the Brooklyn Bridegrooms); the Navy Yard
(closed in 1966, after 150 years of operation but resurrected as an
industrial park, and now slated to be the site of an immense tele-
vision and film studio, which, if completed, will be the largest on
the East Coast); the 1776 Battle of Brooklyn; the Brooklyn Acad-
emy of Music (opened in 1859); the *Monitor;* Brooklyn College,
home of a strong MFA program in creative writing; the Brooklyn
Public Library with its branches in each of the sprawling, idiosyn-
cratic neighborhoods, which represent nearly every nationality,
religion, and creed, and which, according to the U.S. Census Bu-
reau, in 2003 contained an estimated 2,472,523 people. As a char-
acter in Thomas Wolfe's *Death to Morning* said in a fairly accurate
approximation of the borough's famous Brooklynese, "It'd take a
lifetime to know Brooklyn t'roo and t'roo. And even den, you
wouldn't know it all." Wolfe said, too, that only the dead know
Brooklyn, and beyond the portion of its geography devoted to
cemeteries, perhaps he would have been charmed to know that
the first Reformed Dutch Church of the Flatlands was built over
an ancient Canarsie burial ground, and that the Dutch buried
their dead there as well, mingling the remains of both the natives
and the invaders.

Keenly aware of the impossibility of knowing all of the bor-
ough, we promised to keep an eye toward the imaginary Brook-
lyn, Ferlinghetti's "Coney Island of the Mind," the side of the
story that natives and visitors tell to say something distinctive
about the place, something that may not be strictly true, narra-
tive, moral, fashionable, or just back from the dry cleaner. We
chose to include good and great poems that made even fleeting
but compelling reference to Brooklyn, or used Brooklyn as a
starting line, or considered Brooklyn as a symbolic entity—like
Agha Shahid Ali's ghazal imitating Hart Crane, Frank O'Hara's
"Ave Maria," and Tony Towle's "The Allegorical Figure of Brook-
lyn." One Brooklyn is the paradise of Hayden Carruth's hyacinth
garden, another the grisly receptacle of Harvey Shapiro's "Na-
tional Cold Storage Company."

Of course, the Coney Island of the body is here too, in, to
name a few examples, Sara Teasdale's desolate aubade and Maggie

Nelson's charming, last-minute excursion to the Mermaid Parade. Like the bridge, the permanent carnival of Coney Island has tattooed itself on the American imagination—if the first is a passageway, then the latter, named for the rabbits the Dutch spotted in the dunes, is the glowing exit, the electrifying escape. Here, Quentin Rowan transplants Prometheus, and Joanna Furhman imports Freud (who actually visited the site, which he believed to be the unconscious of America), though he never gets to see Dreamland because like the Luna Park in Galway Kinnell's poem, it's already burning. Brooklyn is a place as elusive as the Hell Freud imagines.

Appropriately, to get from the bridge to Coney Island, one must often go underground, through the entire spectrum of emotion and culture. Beneath Bath Beach, Bay Ridge, Bedford-Stuyvesant, Bensonhurst, Bergen Beach, Boreum Hill, Brighton Beach, Brooklyn Heights, Brownsville, Bushwick, Canarsie, Cobble Hill, Coney Island, Crown Heights, Cypress Hills, Downtown Brooklyn, DUMBO, Dyker Heights, East Flatbush, East New York, Flatbush, Flatlands, Fort Greene, Gerritsen Beach, Gowanus, Gravesend, Greenpoint, Kensington and Parkville, Manhattan Beach, Marine Park, Mill Basin, Park Slope, Prospect Heights, Prospect-Lefferts Gardens, Prospect Park South, Red Hook, Sea Gate, Sheepshead Bay, Sunset Park, Williamsburg, Windsor Terrace, and others.

These neighborhoods, named or unnamed, emerge through the Brooklyn poet's genius for memorable particulars. The Romeo in John Wakeman's beautiful dialogue-poem "Love in Brooklyn" might blow his nose after professing his love to Horowitz, but his trembling fingers suggest an awkward, moving sincerity. In "Sunday Morning Café," Alicia Jo Rabins contemplates desire and beauty among the "mosaic of Sunday papers" at the Tea Lounge in Park Slope. Elsewhere, the Dutch scientist and poet Leo Vroman calls the boom boxes of Sheepshead Bay "black coffins full / of unbearably loud singing," and the speaker in Anthony Lacavaro's "The Old Italian Neighborhood" laments the exhaustion of new parenthood while imagining an evening when God can grant dispensations for video-rental late fees; all the same, the poet passes buildings he believes are inhabited by "angry babies, / so many new and angry babies anxious to flood / the morning streets." But release is exactly what Frank O'Hara proposes in "Ave Maria": "Mothers of America / let your kids go the movies!" At the movies, the children of America may find their way not only to "glamorous" countries but to "their first sexual experience" at an "apartment . . . in the / Heaven on Earth Bldg / near the Williamsburgh Bridge." Experience, sexual and otherwise, cannot be avoided, O'Hara seems to tell us. Or in the words of the Chicago community organizer Saul Alinsky: "[H]e who fears corruption fears life." From Walt Whitman's "Sun-down Poem" to Melissa Beattie-Moss, whose "After Making Love" reminds us of the etymology of the word Brooklyn, as well as the tenuousness of safety and love, here are poems that fearlessly celebrate experience but are keenly aware of the passage of time. Flying a kite in Camden, the aged Whitman in Michael Morse's "Suburbia" can't help remembering the "smoke and mirrors" Brooklyn of his childhood.

When Randall Jones at the Center for American Places invited us to put this anthology together, we made a pact to guard against nostalgia and cloying tribute, the sincere poetry Wilde warned us about. Through the resources at the New York Public Library and the hard work and clever acquisitions of Amanda Kole, via the interlibrary loan department of The Pennsylvania State University, as well as the riches waiting to be found at Poets House and The Academy of American Poets, the borough became to us, through the sheer number of poets for whom it was an occasional or sustaining muse, more than the sum of its neighborhoods. The later labor of tracking and negotiating copyright was managed by poet Cynthia Clem, and the Institute for Arts and Humanities at Penn State granted funds for permissions. Michael J. Runyan and Claudia Rankine provided editorial assistance at the project's hectic conclusion. Finally, at NYU Press, thanks to Puja Telikicherla and Despina Papazoglou Gimbel. Throughout this process, one of our criteria was to present poems that capture the physical place itself, which meant hunting poetic portraits of as many neighborhoods and representative cultures as possible, poems that were not content to stand still, that not just offered "recollection in tranquility" but also juggled life's unwieldy luggage.

Brooklyn has a lively biography recorded in the Brooklyn Historical Society (which was, unfortunately, closed for renovation during the gathering process of this anthology), but often we found ourselves drawn to the histories that had been shuttled from somewhere else: history atop history. In Enid Dame's "Soup," the stubborn, lively cook is also the survivor who reminds us that her recipe is no facile domestic feat—her nourishment is a combination of the Vilna Ghetto and her own steadfast dedication to survival. Just because the soup is made in Brighton Beach decades after the Holocaust, ensures no escape or pat conclusion. Her daughter is overwhelmed by the secrets she's been protected from: "Mama, why didn't you tell me?"

Although food is not explicitly named in George Oppen's "Street," the poem confronts us with a skeletal diagram of hunger and impoverishment. The speaker is an avenue onto himself, a host to the disenfranchised on Bergen Street and a witness to the "real pain" they experience, but the poem's true power is that its stark, malnourished lines circle around a bleak conclusion: there is the expectation of improvement harbored by the innocents on their way to degradation, and there is the speaker whose concept of poverty, which amounts to ineffectual sympathy, can achieve no comfort or cure. Similarly, the speaker's childhood home in Donna Masini's "Getting Out of Where We Came From," is built not on a firm foundation but on a swamp. D. Nurkse, a recent poet laureate of Brooklyn (an office conceived of, and originally occupied by, Norman Rosten), delivers a disturbing portrait of police brutality during the Rudolph Giuliani era. And dating from the early 1970s, from Hutch Waters's chapbook *Africa in Brooklyn,* we found "Unpaid Bills," which together with the aching beauty of June Jordan's "For Michael Angelo Thompson" and Audre Lorde's "Cables to Rage," point to the essential social milestones of that era: feminism, civil rights, and the rise of the Black Power and Black Arts movements.

Broken Land is not a stab at historical redress or reconciliation; we concerned ourselves primarily with lyric poems of the twentieth and post-twentieth century, while also making an attempt to represent some interesting poetic precedents to Whitman. By arranging the poems according to publication date, we concerned ourselves with how the borough has been interpreted and represented over time. We limited ourselves to work written for the page, rather than for performance or other media. In our present era of widespread conservatism and convenient catchwords like "homeland security," we can take some solace in thriving poetic communities in New York and other places that offer opportunities for voices that take us far afield from the received notions and the distortions of an increasingly technological, mediated, and impersonal language. Contemporary Brooklyn has abounded in reading series and literary venues: each spring, the Brooklyn Poetry Outreach, organized by Brooklyn Borough President Marty Markowitz and Brooklyn Poet Laureate Ken Siegelman, gathers amateur and professional poets in an open-mike setting; Brooklyn College's "Day of the Poet," also supported by the Brooklyn Borough President's Office, allows high-school-age poets in the borough to work with experienced teachers, work that culminates in performance and publication. In the past decade, establishments such as Brooklyn Moon, Barbès, Pete's Candy Store, Softskull Press, Hanging Loose Press, Halycon Reading Series, and many others have introduced new voices while showcasing well-known authors. Consider the reading series at Pete's Candy Store: originally an Italian candy store and illegal gambling den, the place is now a chic Williamsburg outlet for emerging and established poets. If you're ever off the Lorimer Street stop on the L line on a Monday night, you must walk past the Brooklyn-Queens Expressway to get there. The café is not conspicuous from the outside, but go to the back room, a combination of a vaudeville stage and a railroad room, where you'll find the performance space where, it is said, the illegal gamblers once made their bets.

All good poetry is a gamble, and poems of place don't always pay off. Ezra Pound insisted that it was important that great poems get written, but it was not important who wrote them. Perhaps we can add it's also of no importance *where* they were written. But for a borough that's lived in the shadow of Manhattan and in the more recent shadow of September 11, Brooklyn has produced an astonishing number of poets willing to risk their luck on the place—and if we can count the players at the table, it seems like there's much more to be won before the joint closes.

II. Borough of Churches
Julia Spicher Kasdorf

Heard:

(Lance Henson—
Oklahoma Cheyenne)

How can any self-respecting
Mohawk
live in a place
like this?

Response:
I burn Cedar and Sage
and keep
an eye
on the bridge.

(the final section from
Last Mornings in Brooklyn, Maurice Kenny)

How I came to this place—the Borough, the Bridge, Brighton
Beach, this book—is how I came to be a writer, I now believe. My
myth of origins, like that of many Americans, goes back to Brook-
lyn. As a 21-year-old from Pennsylvania, I transferred from a
small, Mennonite liberal arts college in Indiana to NYU, having
never visited the school. This was 1983, before the East Side
dorms, when NYU undergraduates didn't expect much and
mostly rode in on the train. I took a room at Menno House, on
East 19th Street, a holdover from the days when conscientious
objectors fulfilled their 1-W service at Bellevue. From my bed on
the third floor, I once lay down and visualized every hard surface
between my body and the earth, and wept. Homesick for sky, I'd
hop the F train at West Fourth and ride to the sea. In November,
in sweaters, I once watched two ancient, ferocious women clad in
only their bras and girdles stride out of the surf at Brighton,
doubtless dreaming of Odessa.

Much as I hated it, New York held me. Raised in a community
that once called itself "the quiet in the land," I needed the City's

noise and loud voices. "Anyone might talk to you in New York, anyone does anything right in your face, everything is in the open, and a poetry adequate to New York is OPEN," Alice Notley wrote with regard to Ted Berrigan's work and what it meant for him to write in the City. Brooklyn could only be more so. Two days after I moved to Fort Greene, as I ushered at a Shakespeare performance in Prospect Park, a thwarted boyfriend stabbed his rival in the groin under the band shell during the show. That was 1985—before Spike moved in and the plywood came off the windows on South Oxford Street. I said, "No thank you," every day to the same man who offered to sell me "smoke" as I climbed up from the G-train. Once I dared a shopkeeper to sell me yams and bananas from the window of his store that fronted for something else. It took a lot of energy to sustain such foolishness. And after a year, I married my sweetheart and moved farther out, to the top of a two-family house on Kermit Place, just off Church Avenue, between Concy Island Avenue and Ocean Parkway.

In "Kensington," a name coined by realtors for a section of old Flatbush, I grew to love Brooklyn—and because of it, New York. Old-timers on the block, nostalgic for the borough's heydays in the 1950s, still raged about the Dodgers' desertion and Robert Moses' foul highway wrecking the landscape. They called Manhattan "the city" and almost never went there except to see "a show" with grandchildren growing up on Long Island. They called us yuppies, although my husband and I taught Catholic school or were students ourselves. Carmine, the butcher, told me he followed in his father's line of work because it gave him a chance to talk with women all day. He lamented the working wife who has no time to cook real food or flirt. He lamented TV dinners and all manner of frozen food. When you ordered a cut of anything, he'd ask how you planned to fix it, and if he didn't approve, he'd offer a better recipe, sometimes thrusting fresh parsley into your hand. His advice: it is more important to buy an expensive bottle of olive oil than an expensive bottle of wine. He once asked me to describe Pennsylvania—which he had never seen and imagined only as "The Poconos"—what did it look like, and was it true that people shot and ate deer there? Although pigs' feet and ears began to appear in his cases, he lamented people from the Islands who drifted up Church Avenue from Flatbush. "They eat bones! How can you eat bones?" Afraid of their recipes, unable to converse with those cooks, he fled the neighborhood before I left, moving on to Bay Ridge where, he said, people still eat meat.

In Manhattan, in graduate school, I learned to be cosmopolitan, secular, circumspect, but in Brooklyn everyone seemed marked by tribe and creed, inscribed by the distances they had come. Manhattan demanded a chic hybridity, but the borough of churches was more like the Balkans in the late 1980s and early '90s. Lethal collisions of culture and race erupted in Bensonhurst and Crown Heights, and it was rumored that a true Messiah—from Boro Park, Brooklyn—was dying in an eastside Manhattan hospital, but not forever. For a Mennonite girl whose father grew up in a community so oppositional it still plowed with horses, the place felt like a home, or many homes stuck close together, stinking of foreign foods and strange gods. One year, Good Friday fell on the first night of Passover, and I got swept into the swarm on Church Avenue, everyone shopping and rushing home to cook and pray—except, perhaps, our next-door neighbors, the gracious Chinese family from Burma with a bright, young son named Elvis.

Queens may be the true borough of immigrants, but in my mind, Brooklyn is this: everything and everywhere all at once heading someplace else, dragging whatever is portable from the old place, lucky that most days no one gets killed. Chaotic—beyond certain wealthier sections near the Park and the River. For some of us, Brooklyn remains a place between America and New York City, which is to say the world; for immigrants and émigrés, Brooklyn is the place between the homelands and the United States. Most summer Saturdays, I caught the city bus that glides down Coney Island Avenue through Sabbath-silent Midwood to Brighton, and there found my peace on a noisy, littered beach. Thus my pleasure in discovering Lady Moody, who traveled from Great Britain to colonial Salem seeking religious and personal liberty; finding New England as intolerant as the Old World, she finally settled on a portion of Flatbush Plantation. There she welcomed dissenters—Quakers and Dutch Mennonites among them—in defiance of the Calvinist church. Her house is preserved at Gravesend. It pleases me to think that Mennonites were on Coney Island before the publication of *Martyr's Mirror,* a seventeenth-century compendium of execution and torture that still functions as a grim emblem of identity and remains the community's most important literary work.

Eight years in Kensington was long enough for me to write and publish a first book of poems—mostly about a valley of reserved people in Pennsylvania—and long enough to find a profession. During my seemingly endless studies at NYU, I met Michael Tyrell, a smart but soft-spoken undergraduate who wore only black and read poems like a shark. I admired his poetry, which seemed more intense and wiser than his years, and recognized a restless edge that suggested he would keep moving. At the same time, I got to know a group of varied and unassuming Brooklyn writers; several of whom are included in this anthology: D. Nurkse, and Enid Dame and Donald Lev of *The Home Planet News,* the venerable literary tabloid devoted to the expression of Jewish, feminist, and politically progressive views. (Only after her death did I learn that Enid Dame—the Brooklyn poet—was born in Beaver Falls, Pennsylvania, not far from where I grew up.) And I became affiliated with Poetlink, a group of poets that sponsored readings in Brooklyn venues; of these, Steve Hartman and his Pinched Nerve Press come to mind, as do Nancy Bengis Friedman and her workshop, Barbara Elovic, Phyllis Capello, Melody Davis, and Steve Fried. We held a reading to celebrate the borough in a karate studio in Sunset Heights, another in the Picnic House at Prospect Park; invariably, at those events someone would say, "You'll never see something like this in Queens!" Behind our house on Kermit Place, in one unpaved strip, I tended a gaudy bed of flowers, allowing free rein to the tiny magenta petunias that grow wild in Brooklyn; now I think this collection of poems must be a bit like that bed: unruly, eclectic, loud.

In the end, our New Jersey landlord who had grown up in the house sold out to a Pakistani family, and we had to move on in the early 1990s. As for the next place—Luquer Street, on the last block before the Brooklyn-Queens Expressway—I could praise flowers and pampered fig trees, brownstones and big sycamores, and the outrageous Christmas decorations of Carroll Gardens; Italian-speaking grocers who resembled princes in Florentine paintings, shrines on Court Street dedicated to blind Lucy and the gorgeous black-robed Madonna who was borne through the streets once a year and tipped to bless benefactors' buildings, or the independent video rental with a special section reserved for "Woody, Spike and Jim." But we stayed there for only a couple of years before a job pulled me back to America. What stays with me now from that neighborhood are the pigeons catching late afternoon light on their wings as they circled above Clinton Street every day before vanishing into their rooftop cages, what they call "homing."

A friend told me of a time he was so depressed and dissatisfied with his work that he traveled from his Brooklyn studio to look at a certain wonderful painting at the art museum in Newark, New Jersey. Wandering through the galleries afterward, he came upon a room full of mediocre pictures executed in dated twentieth-century academic style, and on the curator's labels, nearly all carried the same haunting refrain: "born: Vienna, Austria, died: Brooklyn, NY . . . born: Paris, France, died: Brooklyn, NY . . . born: Vilna, Latvia, died: Brooklyn, NY." Then he resolved to change his work and change his life, or at least—so he wouldn't end up "born: Shanghai, China, died: Brooklyn, NY—he decided to move! Of course, mobility comes with money and a little nerve. It takes another kind of nerve to stick around.

JULIA SPICHER KASDORF

On Leaving Brooklyn
1998

After Psalm 137

If I forget thee
let my tongue forget the songs
it sang in this strange land
and my heart forget the secrets
only a stranger can learn.
Borough of churches, borough of crack,
if I forget how ailanthus trees sprout
on the rooftops, how these streets
end in water and light,
let my eyes grow nearsighted.
Let my blood forget
the map of its travels
and my other blood cease
its slow tug toward the sea
if I do not remember,
if I do not always consider thee
my Babylon, my Jerusalem.

III. Exits from Brooklyn
Michael Tyrell

> . . . No cold War, no economic slump
> Could touch us in that Brooklyn; the word itself
> seems holy,
> a Cabalistic lunchbox
> Yawning open for all the world . . .
>
> —Noelle Kocot, "Brooklyn Sestina 1975"

For my first seven years, I had the privilege of living in two cities: Brooklyn and Manhattan. Well, in a sense. My family (a single mother, her parents, and I) lived on Manhattan Avenue in Greenpoint, Brooklyn, a short walk from the parish of St. Anthony and St. Alphonsus. From the window that faced Manhattan Avenue, the neighborhood's main drag, I had my earliest view of commerce: Cheap Charlie's Discount Store, Trunz Fish Market, Paris Shoe Store, a catering hall where the cousins had their wedding receptions. (In my extended family, the seventies were all about weddings and funerals; the eighties were just about funerals.)

Greenpoint is known today as the largest Polish community in New York City, but in the late seventies, most of the signs were still in English, though *Apteka* would soon overtake Pharmacy; *Ksiegarnia,* Bookstore. It was probably at that window that I learned to put letters and words together, where the alphabet became more than a series of streets—Ash, Box, Clay, Dupont, Eagle, Freeman, and so on—at the northern tip of the neighborhood.

Before I could read signage or language, my grandmother and mother taught me the art of people-reading: how to spot their friends en route to the bingo or the penny social, because these women wore bright, clean blouses and always seemed weighed down by the burden and joy of bargain-hunting. There were other signals people gave off, signals I could pick up from that view. I learned, for example, to recognize the sluggish, stuttering walk of junkies, who seemed to sleepwalk by day and claim doorways by night.

People, I felt, were easy to read; I had them all figured out by the time I was four years old. People moved; you read them, which prompted you to wave to them or ignore them. They materialized, they came and went, they vanished into buildings, they emerged and vanished again. Language was different, something that seemed to move and stand still, even stutter and sleepwalk, all at the same time. Odd, for instance, how those sales posters in the discount stores would get barred up after dark, but a sentence my grandmother or mother uttered, about their shopper friends—*Look at them, going out gallivanting*—seemed to hang in the air long after it was said.

As soon as I could grasp the concept, I loved the idea of living on a street called Manhattan that was not part of Manhattan. I marveled at how a place could be changed just by naming it. It was like seeing a ship inside a bottle, a skyline inside a snow globe.

I learned other things from the view. The clock in the tall steeple of St. Anthony and St. Alphonsus taught me how to tell time. This was done best at night, when the glowing clock face stood out like a permanent full moon. When I was very young, I hated watches, no matter what cartoon character showed up on them. What bothered me was the second hand: time jumping almost too fast to count. God seemed to need only an hour hand and a minute hand, so I trusted His method. At night, I wasn't allowed to sit by the street-facing window for very long, so I had to learn my lessons about time quickly, but the two women in my life allowed me to look out the back window, which had a magnificent view of the Twin Towers, at the time only a few years older than I.

After my grandmother and grandfather died, time seemed to speed up. I started wearing watches; teachers and other kids complicated all my neat conclusions about human nature. I went to school and my mother worked, so except for the dog, the apartment was empty most of the day. My mother worked in a dress shop. All her life, she was an expert on two things: clothes and bargains. She could tell you, for example, which top could hide a pregnancy, which five-and-dime would give you the best deal on cigarettes.

It's 1981. It's a spring afternoon, but no leaves have come out yet. It's mild enough for teenagers to practically dry-hump on the benches in McCarren Park, but the weather hasn't fully decided that it's spring yet. There's some smutty snow tucked between the columns of the bank, there are weather forecasters who say there might be a light snowfall in the next few days. In my mother's shop, the displays are all about the summer, a season people aren't ready to buy.

Business is slow, so my mother gets to go home early. I'm still at school.

When she comes in the apartment, she finds that the dog's locked up in the bathroom, locked up and barking.

In the living room she finds the explanation for the dog's agitation and imprisonment: the lanky man wearing a cross and an I HEART·NY T-shirt, she'll say later. They stop and study each other. It's almost as if he's deciding whether he's really a burglar, almost as if she's mulling over whether this is really her apartment anymore, or if she's walked into the wrong one, where this person is the rightful tenant. There are some resemblances between them. She carries a shopping bag full of bargains, clothes bought at a discount at her shop; he carries a shopping bag packed with my grandmother's costume jewelry and our ancient stereo.

The man doesn't say anything. My mother drops her bags and charges.

At the age of nine, my mother was the best fistfighter in her family—she could beat up her brothers because brothers didn't scratch and bite, the way sisters did. At fourteen, my mother told a mother superior to go to hell (and so goodbye, Catholic school); at twenty-five she met the movie star John Garfield, who stepped out of a car in Manhattan and mistook her for someone else; at forty-two she successfully concealed a pregnancy from everyone and never told anyone who the father was. This man is not on the same level as those challenges; this is only a burglar. She drops her bags and charges. She's from Brooklyn, and so she has the confidence that she can kick anyone's ass. No thought about weapons he might be carrying; no worries about what might happen. The women in my family are like this: ass-kickers. They smoke, they curse, they shop, they attack. When my godmother's son told his mother that she was killing him with her incessant smoking, my godmother, my first cousin and a fellow Greenpointer, snapped at him: "These cigarettes are the only thing keeping me from kicking your ass."

My mother was lucky because she was unharmed. The burglar had no weapons. He pushed her aside, fending off her curses and

her fists, but he didn't hurt her. She didn't kick his ass, but she
succeeded in getting him running out the front door. Our burglar
was so surprised, he left behind the shopping bag which had a
smaller bag inside it, his burglar kit—a crowbar, a Phillips screw-
driver, a hat to cover his face, a bottle of cheap whiskey maybe to
work up his nerve. My mother and the dog chased him down the
stairs, but they lost him on the street. Then my mother collared
the dog, a brindled pit bull mix, who she said had probably been
maced by the burglar. The dog was coming out of his trance and
was barking and trembling, ready for a long chase. She said later
that she didn't want him to get hit by a car. She started to tremble
a bit herself, something she said she noticed when she pulled the
dog back into the building. When they reached the top of the
stairs, she noticed the lock on the apartment door was broken.
Later that day, by the time I'd been picked up at school, my
mother's brother, Honeyboy, had come to fix the lock.

But her confidence was broken—invaders could get in, some of
our family had been robbed three or four times. Like them, my
mother chose flight.

A move to Long Island followed, a decade when Manhattan
was no longer the avenue I lived on, and its borough namesake no
longer a subway ride away.

Long before I read poems, long before I thought I'd have to
write them, I tried to come up with shortcuts back to Brooklyn,
or to any metropolitan environment, which usually meant read-
ing every book I could get my hands on and watching every city-
related movie and program broadcast on TV. I resolved to get
away from a life in Long Island as soon as I had something to say
about it. That plan always seemed to revolve around a return to
Brooklyn. But my mother and I had no money to waste on trips
back to visit the ones who had stayed behind; only funerals earned
us those visits.

As far as feeding the imagination, Long Island was no Proustian
miracle; the smell of manicured grass was a world removed from
the fish-market stink of my first street. I never learned to love
what I had—danger abstracted as patches of undeveloped, wooded
land, safety concretized as the sign with the big eyeball that said
"Neighborhood Watch"—much as the life I thought I could be liv-
ing in Brooklyn. Long Island felt like a life without a view.

Beyond my own sketchy cache of memories of Brooklyn and my mother's stories of growing up in Greenpoint during the Depression and the Second World War, the iceman, her grandmother the undertaker's assistant, my grandfather the German veteran who fought against the Germans, the house inherited by an aunt from a descendant of Abraham Lincoln's secretary of war, there were those images I glimpsed in popular culture, some of them comic or poignant, that kept me anchored to Brooklyn: Ralph and Alice Kramden's dingy kitchen in Bensonhurst; Cher, in the movie *Moonstruck*, in love kicking a can near the Promenade; other movies, like *On the Waterfront* and *A Tree Grows in Brooklyn;* and later, most crucially, *Last Exit to Brooklyn,* in both its literary and cinematic forms.

Perhaps no other portrait of Brooklyn compelled me as much as Selby's—it brought me back to the borough, but it terrified me. The characters in it suffered greatly, but no two suffered alike: the teenage prostitute and the unwed mother, the homosexual union organizer and the neighborhood transvestite—no restored locks, no flight, was possible for them. No one in the story ended up happy, few got out alive or sane, but when I read and watched *Last Exit,* I discovered something akin to what I'd discover in poetry a few years later: a view that seemed to be what Brooklyn was, a frame that could contain God, burglars, bargain-hunters, and the complexities of language and pathos themselves. I never once pretended that my own feeling of being stranded (wasn't I only two hours away—and a few elusive dollars—from where I wanted to go?) was on the same level as the gang rape, beatings, riots, and other violence that coursed through the book and film, or even on the same level as my easy judgments made at the window facing Manhattan Avenue. What struck me for the first time was that suffering could be almost lyrical when gracefully, pitilessly expressed, not glossed over or ignored. What I found there was not so much identification but an idea of a place where no character, no matter what his or her fate, could be ignored. I held on to this idea. Of course, I didn't want to imitate those lives, but I was glad to be reminded that they had a right to exist. When I began reading poems at the end of high school and I made my first attempts to write them, I think I asked of poetry an identical intensity. To some degree on both ends, the demand was satisfyingly answered.

It never occurred to me to write a poem about Brooklyn until long after I got to New York University, which predictably proved my best exit from Long Island. There, I met and studied with the encouraging and brilliant Julia Kasdorf, whose poems I admired for many reasons, perhaps most of all their remarkably strong sense of place. It was an element largely absent from my own work, and for a long time I resisted naming the locations of my speakers and environments. What impressed me about Julia's poems was that they seemed exceptional to my prejudice about place; they were firmly located not only in her native Pennsylvania and the Mennonite community into which she was born but also in Brooklyn, her adopted community. They seemed to me neither sentimental nor nostalgic but as subtly incisive as they were musically vibrant; hers was a speaker alert to her surroundings but not narcotized by them.

In my senior year of college, I lived in Brooklyn again, but only briefly, in the house my aunt inherited from the descendant of Lincoln's secretary of war, a house rumored to be haunted. All of it should have proved interesting source material; Julia predicted that I would write good poems about my "homecoming." It would take a year for her prediction to come true, and true to my tendency to write about a place only after I'd left it, it happened in Lewisburg, Pennsylvania, where I was staying at a retreat for young poets. In the end, only one respectable poem emerged on the subject, a piece about St. Anthony's church (although I forgot to put in the second saint's name—an omission of memory, or an homage to my mother, who still petitions the saint of lost things). It was probably the first poem I wrote where I claimed something of Brooklyn as my own, and it felt, in its own small way, like the most important homecoming of all.

As I write this, it's July 2003 in the Bushwick section of Brooklyn, and the fudgesicle truck is jingling down Troutman Street; every day the theme from *The Sting* wanders insistently among the familiar Brooklyn hollers, gushing hydrants, and sirens. Down the block from my railroad apartment, a homemade memorial has been mounted for a twenty-year-old, dead of an overdose. In front of a closed storefront, once the dead guy's favorite hangout, before that a Baptist church, sits an open cardboard box containing Santeria candles and a few loose Newports.

R. I. P. LITO, MY LITTLE NIGGAH, written in white shoe polish, emblazons several windshields. The salon called "Beautyrama" has been closed for months, but the auto parts store known as "Affordable Collision" endures. I have one more day here in Bushwick (which the cheerleaders of gentrification have been calling "East Williamsburg" in the *Voice* ads) where I've been living for eighteen months, one more month in New York until I leave the state for a another writer's retreat, this one in Connecticut.

Like a few Manhattanites I know, unlike no Long Islanders I know, I have no driver's license. Recently, I've been taking lessons to change that—I feel like an overgrown boy who still makes his turns too sharp and honks at pigeons who seem thoroughly used to having the industrial streets of Bushwick all to themselves. My driver's ed. instructor tells me there's no better place to learn how to drive because "you'll never see more aggressive motherfuckers." He said that that was his take on the line from the song "New York, New York," the famous lines that talk about survival in New York, how it prepares you for any place you might go. I want to pass the test most people half my age pass. More than that, I just hope all my .collisions are affordable, no exit from Brooklyn my last.

MICHAEL TYRELL

Against Angels
1997

> *Bright souls without a seam.*
> —*Rainer María Rilke, "The Angels"*

In the stained glass of St. Anthony's church,
they flew too perfectly, arriving everywhere,
like guests who never decline invitation,
outlasting their welcome, gossips
in gardens, mangers, temples, at any eventful site
where their golden wings would be
superfluous, and Lucifer's example
the notable absence, the reminder
how paradise gets lost every day on earth.
Named for the archangel, I walked
each Sunday under the raised swords
of the seraphs and wondered what bribery,
what innocence could earn the blond hair
and blinding haloes ascending to countries of clouds,
what barter to molt my body
and again touch the body of my father?
The legends of Joan and Sebastian,
the priest insisted: feathers shot from their shoulders,
each became identical,
not in size but character, no true sex,
none desiring touch or favoring
silence over music. And, as I hunted the ceiling
for a proof of their human lives, I found
nothing, not a single arrow, I saw each hovering god
no different than the stone-faced images
guarding local graves, their open hands
not a welcome into light
but a gesture of dismissal,
a rejection of the body that stood against
the wings on those windows,
and the iron bars behind them.

PART I

Crossing Brooklyn Ferry

Walt Whitman

WALT WHITMAN

Sun-down Poem

1855–1865

Flood-tide of the river, flow on! I watch you, face to face,
Clouds of the west! sun half an hour high! I see you also
    face to face.

Crowds of men and women attired in the usual costumes,
    how curious you are to me!
On the ferry-boats the hundreds and hundreds that cross
    are more curious to me than you suppose,
And you that shall cross from shore to shore years hence, are more
    to me, and more in my meditations, than you might suppose.

The impalpable sustenance of me from all things at all hours of
    the day,
The simple, compact, well-joined scheme—myself disintegrated,
    every one disintegrated, yet part of the scheme,
The similitudes of the past and those of the future,
The glories strung like beads on my smallest sights and hearings—
    on the walk in the street, and the passage over the river,
The current rushing so swiftly, and swimming with me far away,
The others that are to follow me, the ties between me and them,
The certainty of others—the life, love, sight, hearing of others.

Others will enter the gates of the ferry, and cross from shore to
    shore,
Others will watch the run of the flood-tide,
Others will see the shipping of Manhattan north and west,
    and the heights of Brooklyn to the south and east,
Others will see the islands large and small,
Fifty years hence others will see them as they cross, the sun
    half an hour high,
A hundred years hence, or ever so many hundred years hence,
    others will see them,
Will enjoy the sun-set, the pouring in of the flood-tide, the
    falling back
        to the sea of the ebb-tide.

It avails not, neither time or place—distance avails not,
I am with you, you men and women of a generation,
    or ever so many generations hence,
I project myself, also I return—I am with you, and know how it is.

Just as you feel when you look on the river and sky, so I felt,
Just as any of you is one of a living crowd, I was one of a crowd,
Just as you are refreshed by the gladness of the river,
    and the bright flow, I was refreshed,
Just as you stand and lean on a rail, yet hurry with the swift current,
    I stood, yet was hurried,
Just as you look on the numberless masts of ships,
    and the thick-stemmed pipes of steamboats, I looked.

I too many and many a time crossed the river, the sun half an
        hour high,
I watched the December sea-gulls, I saw them high in the air
        floating
    with motionless wings oscillating their bodies,
I saw how the glistening yellow lit up parts of their bodies,
    and left the rest in strong shadow,
I saw the slow-wheeling circles and the gradual edging toward
        the south.

I too saw the reflection of the summer-sky in the water,
Had my eyes dazzled by the shimmering track of beams,
Looked at the fine centrifugal spokes of light round the shape
    of my head in the sun-lit water,
Looked on the haze on the hills southward and southwestward,
Looked on the vapor as it flew in fleeces tinged with violet,
Looked toward the lower bay to notice the arriving ships,
Saw their approach, saw aboard those that were near me,
Saw the white sails of schooners and sloops, saw the ships at
        anchor,
The sailors at work in the rigging or out astride the spars,
The round masts, the swinging motion of the hulls,
    the slender serpentine pennants,
The large and small steamers in motion, the pilots in their
        pilot-houses,

The white wake left by the passage, the quick tremulous whirl
    of the wheels,

The flags of all nations, the falling of them at sun-set,
The scallop-edged waves in the twilight, the ladled cups,
    the frolicsome crests and glistening,
The stretch afar growing dimmer and dimmer, the gray walls
    of the granite store-houses by the docks,
On the river the shadowy group, the big steam-tug closely
        flanked
    on each side by the barges—the hay-boat, the belated lighter,
On the neighboring shore the fires from the foundry chimneys
    burning high and glaring into the night,
Casting their flicker of black, contrasted with wild red and yel-
        low light,
    over the tops of houses, and down into the clefts of streets.

These and all else were to me the same as they are to you,
I project myself a moment to tell you—also I return.

I loved well those cities,
I loved well the stately and rapid river,
The men and women I saw were all near to me,
Others the same—others who look back on me, because I looked
    forward to them,
The time will come, though I stop here today and tonight.

What is it, then, between us? What is the count of the scores
    or hundreds of years between us?
Whatever it is, it avails not—distance avails not, and place
    avails not.

I too lived,
I too walked the streets of Manhattan Island, and bathed in the
    waters around it;
I too felt the curious abrupt questionings stir within me,
In the day, among crowds of people, sometimes they came
    upon me,
In my walks home late at night, or as I lay in my bed, they
    came upon me.

I too had been struck from the float forever held in solution,
I too had received identity by my body,
That I was, I knew was of my body, and what I should be,
   I knew I should be of my body.

It is not upon you alone the dark patches fall,
The dark threw patches down upon me also,
The best I had done seemed to me blank and suspicious,
My great thoughts, as I supposed them, were they not in reality
      meagre?
   Would not people laugh at me?

It is not you alone who know what it is to be evil,
I am he who knew what it was to be evil,
I too knitted the old knot of contrariety,
Blabbed, blushed, resented, lied, stole, grudged,
Had guile, anger, lust, hot wishes I dared not speak,
Was wayward, vain, greedy, shallow, sly, a solitary committer, a
      coward, a malignant person,
The wolf, the snake, the hog, not wanting in me,
The cheating look, the frivolous word, the adulterous wish, not
      wanting,
Refusals, hates, postponements, meanness, laziness, none of
      these wanting.

But I was a Manhattanese, free, friendly, and proud!
I was called by my nighest name by clear loud voices of young men
      as they saw me approaching or passing,
Felt their arms on my neck as I stood, or the negligent leaning
      of their flesh against me as I sat,
Saw many I loved in the street, or ferry-boat, or public assembly,
      yet never told them a word,
Lived the same life with the rest, the same old laughing, gnawing,
      sleeping,
Played the part that still looks back on the actor or actress,
The same old role, the role that is what we make it, as great
      as we like, or as small as we like, or both great and small.

Closer yet I approach you,
What thought you have of me, I had as much of you—

I laid in my stores in advance,
I considered long and seriously of you before you were born.

Who was to know what should come home to me?
Who knows but I am enjoying this?
Who knows but I am as good as looking at you now,
    for all you cannot see me?

It is not you alone, nor I alone,
Not a few races, not a few generations, not a few centuries,
It is that each came, or comes, or shall come, from its due emission,
    without fail, either now, or then, or henceforth.

Every thing indicates—the smallest does, and the largest does,
A necessary film envelops all, and envelops the soul for a proper
        time.

Now I am curious what sight can ever be more stately and
        admirable
    to me than my mast-hemm'd Manhatta, my river and sun-set,
    and my scallop-edged waves of flood-tide, the sea-gulls
    oscillating their bodies, the hay-boat in the twilight,
    and the belated lighter,
Curious what gods can exceed these that clasp me by the hand,
    and with voices I love call me promptly and loudly
    by my nighest name as I approach,
Curious what is more subtle than this which ties me to the woman
    or man that looks in my face,
Which fuses me into you now, and pours my meaning into you.

We understand, then, do we not?
What I promised without mentioning it, have you not accepted?
What the study could not teach—what the preaching could not
    accomplish is accomplished, is it not?
What the push of reading could not start is started by me personally,
    is it not?

Flow on, river! Flow with the flood-tide, and ebb with the ebb-
    tide!
Frolic on, crested and scallop-edged waves!

Gorgeous clouds of the sun-set, drenched with your splendor me,
or the men and women generations after me!
Cross from shore to shore, countless crowds of passengers!
Stand up, tall masts of Manahatta!—stand up, beautiful hills of
Brooklyn!
Bully for you! you proud, friendly, free Manhattanese!
Throb, baffled and curious brain! throw out questions and answers!
Suspend here and everywhere, eternal float of solution!
Blab, blush, lie, steal, you or I or any one after us!
Gaze, loving and thirsting eyes, in the house or street or public
assembly!
Sound out, voices of young men! loudly and musically call me
by my nighest name!
Live, old life! play the part that looks back on the actor or actress!
Play the old role, the role that is great or small, according as one
makes it!
Consider, you who peruse me, whether I may not in
unknown ways be looking upon you!
Be firm, rail over the river, to support those who lean idly, yet haste
with the hasting current!
Fly on, sea-birds! fly sideways, or wheel in large circles high in the
air!
Receive the summer-sky, you water! faithfully hold it till all
downcast eyes
have time to take it from you!
Diverge, fine spokes of light, from the shape of my head,
or any one's head, in the sun-lit water!
Come on, ships from the lower bay! pass up or down,
white-sailed schooners, sloops, lighters!
Flaunt away, flags of all nations! be duly lowered at sun-set!
Burn high your fires, foundry chimneys! cast black shadows at
night-fall!
cast red and yellow light over the tops of houses!
Appearances, now or henceforth, indicate what you are!
You necessary film, continue to envelop the soul!
About my body for me, and your body for you, be hung
our divinest aromas!
Thrive, cities! Bring your freight, bring your shows,
ample and sufficient rivers!

Expand, being than which none else is perhaps more spiritual!
Keep your places, objects than which none else is more lasting!

We descend upon you and all things, we arrest you all,
We realize the soul only by you, you faithful solids and fluids,
Through you color, form, location, sublimity, ideality,
Through you every proof, comparison, and all the suggestions
    and determinations of ourselves.

You have waited, you always wait, you dumb beautiful ministers!
    you novices!
We receive you with free sense at last, and are insatiate hencefor-
    ward,
Not you any more shall be able to foil us, or withhold yourselves
    from us,
We use you, and do not cast you aside—we plant you permanently
    within us,
We fathom you not—we love you—there is perfection in you also,
You furnish your parts toward eternity,
Great or small, you furnish your parts toward the soul.

PART II

Beginnings: Seventeenth, Eighteenth, and Ninetcenth Centuries

Traditional Lenape
Henricus Selyns
Philip Freneau
Joseph L. Chester
W. E. Davenport
John A. Armstrong
Walt Whitman
Anonymous

Prior to the Dutch arrival, the land that is now Brooklyn had been inhabited by Native American people for 11,000 years. Wallam Olum (Red score) is thought to be a translation from the pictograph record of the Lenape. This section was modified and included in a pageant given by the Brooklyn Poetry Circle in "The Story of the Poets of Old Breukelen," at the World's Fair in New York in 1939.

The Wallam Olum, Book One

Part 1—Creation

In the beginning of our time in this far space
Which now surrounds the earth,
There was a great expanse of fog,
Beyond the fog, the Great Creator our Manito abided
He made the land, He made the sky,
He made the sun, the moon, the stars;
He made them all to move in harmony.
He made the wind blow and clear the fog;
The waters flowing far and wide
As islands grew and they remained.
Then wisely thought the Manito, a Manito to Manitoes,
To make a heaven of the earth
For being mortal, souls and all.
He gave them first a mother, a mother
He created,
The mother of all beings
To those very first men, of first of mothers,
He gave them wives.
He brought them food when first they needed it
And gratitude for gratitude.
He gave the fish, He gave the turtle,
He gave the beasts, the birds.
All men had cheerful knowledge, all had leisure,
And all had thoughts of earth in gladness,
And ever after He was Manito to them,
Their children and their children's children.
But secretly an evil being,

A sly magician came upon the earth;
He made the evil beings, he made the evil manito,
He made the evil monsters,
He made the flies, he made the gnats.
He brought with him the badness,
He brought the quarreling and much unhappiness.
He brought the stormy weather;
With sickness—
Brought with him the pain of the end in death.
All this took place upon the earth
And far beyond the great tide waters.
But at the first, before the evil manito had come
All was peaceful, all were friendly.
It was the selfishness of man that brought
This evil unto him.
While wisely, our Manito, the Great!
Great Manito!
"The Manito to Manitoes!" . . .
Is patient, just and kind.

On Mercenary and Unjust Bailiffs

c. 1660

If they true bailiffs be, who for the law maintaining,
    Do orphans overwhelm, and widows terrify,
And hamlets gobble up, the poor with sport disdaining,
    I know not; but, I trow, a schout should ever try
To have the law of God and sovereign rights possess him,
The wrong with power by right and not by wrong suppressing.

Epitaph

FOR MADAM ANNA LOOCKERMANS, WIDOW OF OLOF STEPHENSEN
VAN CORTLANDT, ESQ., DECEASED 14 MAY, 1684.

Here rests who after Cortlandt's death no rest possessed,
    And sought no other rest than soon to rest beside him.
He died. She lived and died. Both now in Abram rest,
    And there, where Jesus is, true rest and joys abide in.
God's will did Anna serve; God's aid did Hannah pray.
    In this alone alike, that both have passed away.

The Market Girl
c. 1776

At dawn of day, from short repose,
At hours that might all townsmen shame,
To catch our money, round or square,
She from the groves of *Flushing* came
With kail and cabbage—fresh and fair.

At *Brooklyn* wharff, in travelling trim,
Arrived an hour before the sun,
Young *Charon's* boat receives her store.
Across the wavy waste they skim;
And thus they, laughing, come to town,
She at the helm, and he, the oar.

Full early taught the arts of gain,
No sharping knave that walks the street,
(Though versed in all the tricks of trade)
No city nymph, or powdered swain,
With all their art, can hope to cheat
A BARGAIN from this country maid.

The market done, her cash secured,
She homeward takes her wonted way:
The painted chest, behind the door,
(With many a GOLDEN GUINEA stored)
Receives the gainings of the day;
Laid up—to see the sun no more!

Sweet nymph! why all this ceaseless pain,
Such early toil, such evening care,
This hoarding for the age to come!
If he that courts you, courts in vain,
And you, regardless of an heir,
Refuse—dear girl, to take him home!

Greenwood Cemetery
1843

The solemn stillness of these grand old woods,
Amid whose labyrinthine paths I roam,
Sinks to the very soul, and so reveals
A language which the heart alone can read.
 This is the land of shadows! Human life,
Save that within my breast, is here unknown.
The silent numbers in the graves beneath
Greet not th' intruder on their peaceful rest;—
Yet few the years since this decaying dust
Was animate, and gladness filled the eyes
That shone in Youth and Beauty. Sunny locks
Lay on those shrunken brows, or softly swept
The cheeks once rosy with the bloom of health.
Around those necks Affection twined its arms,
And pressed the lips where now are lips no more:
And such shall be *my* fate! Think well, my soul!
Art thou prepared to yield this body up,
To be resolved into its native clay,
And mingle with its kind beneath this turf?
Oh! if the parted soul have aught of care
For what hath been its tried companion long,
Methinks it could not choose a fitter spot
For its long dreamless sleep—than this!

 Here is the unshorn forest:—Man, as yet,
Hath not destroyed the handiwork of God.
The hardy oak uplifts his stalwart arms,
Rejoicing in his strength—and by his side
The melancholy aspen waves her boughs,
And makes sad music with her fluttering leaves.
The clinging vine, with its delicious fruit,
And all unpruned, a grateful arbor weaves,—
While flowers, uncultured, breathe on every side,
And spring, luxuriant, from the turf beneath.
 And here are streams, that softly glide along

'Mid verdant banks and shrubs that fringe their shores,
Making a pleasant murmur on their way.
And here are limpid lakes, whose depths reveal
The smooth white pebbles on the sand below.
And here are mountains, easy of ascent,
Whose summits overlook enchanting scenes:—
Most worthily the chief of these maintains
The name of him whom every freeman loves:—
I stand upon Mount WASHINGTON, and gaze
Enraptured on the view within my sight:
The city's spires—its broad and noble bay—
Lie, like a vivid panorama, spread
By master hands in lines of glowing life:—
Turning, the restless ocean meets my eye,
And faintly, when the southern breeze is full,
I hear thy roar, far-sounding Rockaway!

When Winter comes, the arctic winds will howl
Among the rocking boughs, and snows will spread
Their fleecy mantle o'er the summer sward,—
But what have they who sleep to fear? Ere long
The breath of gentle Spring will melt the frost—
Unlock the icy portals of the streams—
And scatter beauty on the withered turf.
Again the flowers shall bloom—again the trees
Put on their garniture of fragrant leaves,
And stand arrayed in flowing robes of life.
So till the end shall come!
                Oh! if to die
Doth fill the parting soul with secret dread,
Methinks she would more willingly depart
Could she but know her consort here would rest.
Already am I half in love with Death!

What feet are entering on my solitude?
I see, by yonder thicket, one who walks
With nervous pace, casting a hasty glance
On every grave that meets his restless eye.
I know him, by the sombre garb he wears,

And by the tell-tale features on his face,
To be a mourner, and, if I may judge,
But late a husband, just returned from sea,
To find that she—whose image he had kept
For months of absence safe within his heart,
And hoped to cherish, when his roving feet
Should bound again upon his native shore—
Is numbered with the breathless host that dwell
In charnel-house and sepulchre! He stops
By yon green mound, and for a moment looks
With anxious eye upon the board that tells
The sleeper's name:—It is the grave he sought,—
And, ere he kneels, he bares his manly brow,
And lifts his clear blue eye to heaven. He speaks—
I'll listen and record his words:—

"And they have laid thee here, dear one, to rest
Far from the turmoil of the distant town,—
Here, where thy blest and beautiful repose
Is not disturbed by shouts of revelry,
Nor the sweet flowers that bloom upon thy grave
Spoiled of their fragrance by unhallowed feet.
I looked not for thy dwelling where arose
In mockery the tall white monument:
Such sign I needed not to tell me where
Thy loved remains reposed. These modest flowers—
The sweet wild-rose and small leaved violet,
Half-hidden by the soft, luxuriant grass—
Are fittest watchers of thy peaceful sleep.
When first I spied them in their hiding-place
My anxious search was ended, for I knew
No *mean* flowers, dearest, from *thy* dust would grow!"

I will no more. 'Tis treason thus to spy
The secret workings of a mourner's grief.
I'll bend my footsteps towards the world again,
And be a graver and a better man.

W. E. DAVENPORT

These Days
c. 1870

What'er they mean to others
To me these days in Brooklyn lived are days of revelation;
Times of the giving of the law, days of eternal judgements;
Days of the truth of man's completion, the union of the race.
Behold! All lands and peoples flow together,
Behold! My city filled with Afric's tribes and Asia's;
Behold! Theologies forgot, old churches and their claims, long
      held, neglected.
Lo! Newer, fitter claims advanced; not those of any class nor cult
      whatever;
Lo! Lo! Beside me here suggesting, whispering, sometimes shout-
      ing clearly,
There is that sure divine reports communicates directly.
What was meant by Jesus Christ stands in modern forms displayed.
And what you mean, O Brooklyn man: Manhattanese or Bronx
      or Queens or Richmond
   dweller,
Here I chant with powerful pride, confessing, testifying.
Who not approves in deeds his love hath witnessed against life.
When faith courts truth, all personal aims walk out like hired
      servants.
For me 'tis enough! I give all! Now content in age my bread I
      take from lovers.
(Nor is what I seek to do for others needful so to perform
More than that in my own person I illustrate my songs,
That my words signify life.)

A Ditty of Greenpoint
1872

Written by SAGITTARIUS, and sung with thrilling effect by Mr. PEELER
(Dec. 1, 1868.) Air.—"The Last Rose of Summer."

'Tis drill-day to-morrow;
We've searched all around,
But search where wc will,
Not a goat's to be found.
Where, where can we pounce on
Some *Nanny* or *Bill,*
To afford us a scape-goat
And save us from drill?

WALT WHITMAN

The Wallabout Martyrs
1888

(*In Brooklyn, in an old vault, mark'd by no special recognition, lie huddled at this moment the undoubtedly authentic remains of the staunchest and earliest Revolutionary patriots from the British prison ships and prisons of the times of 1776–83, in and around New York, and from all over Long Island; originally buried—many thousands of them—in trenches in the Wallabout sands.*)

Greater than memory of Achilles or Ulysses,
More, more by far to thee than tomb of Alexander,
Those cart loads of old charnel ashes, scales and splints of
      mouldy bones,
Once living men—once resolute courage, aspiration, strength,
The stepping stones to thee to-day and here, America.

The Legend of Coney Island, part I
1897

> *Wherein is related a fact of its early history, and which*
> *is supposed to be connected with the disappearance in the*
> *surf, on July 34th [sic], by an unknown and mysterious gentleman.*
> *See papers of that date.*

Part 1

There is no island on the zone,
But has a legend of its own.
Some startling romance of its youth,
Complete in everything but—truth.
But Coney Island's famous mystery
Is true—as any of this history.

T'was told me by an ancient man,
Past many years the allotted span;
Young men may lie, but he was old,
And vouched for every word he told.

'Way back in Coney's early days,
Before Ben Butler, Cox or Hays,
A ruddy Dutchman bore him sway
From Norton's point to Rockaway.
Here, like a patroon, at his ease
He lived, with children at his knees.

Diedrieck Von Smitzerl was his name,
From Amsterdam his forebears came,
And all there was to mar his life,
Were sundry notions of his wife;
For she was active and emphatic,
In striking contrast to her husband,
Who was rather round-cornered and lymphatic.

One day, so runs the thrilling tale,
Frau Smitzerl's appetite did fail
To herrings, sour-krout, wurst and cheese,
Pretzels, zweibake, and things like these,
Bologna and Westphalian hams,
And sent her good man out for clams.

The day was cold, and Smitzerl sighed,
Quite loth to leave the chimney side,
But good Frau Smitzerl's way was winning,
And had been so from the beginning.
So he with bucket and a spade,
Tracks for the nearest clam patch made.

Loud roared the surf, the gulls flew in,
Poor Smitzerl shivered in his skin.

He tried for clams, but they were shy—
The poor man sat him down to cry.
But while he moaned in misery,
His salt tears mingling with the sea,

A mermaid from the wave rose dripping,
And unto Diedrieck's side came tripping,
As mermaids of this later date
Would do to one in such a state.
Into her ears, in accents brief,
Poor Smitzerl poured his clammy grief.

The maiden's tender-heart was torn,
To hear how much poor Dirck had borne.
She clasped his hand, "Come thou with me,"
She cried, "and you a prince shall be;
No longer serve so harsh a Mrs.,
Who calls for *clams* a day like this is."

"I am a princess, and my throne
And coral halls shall be your own.
Then come with me, and we will rule,
And have our lager, always cool."

Poor Smitzerl scratched his head and turned,
To where his distant ingle burned.
He saw Frau Smitzerl at the door—
Frau Smitzerl saw him never more.

What happened when they went below,
My old informant didn't now;
Until one day, come twenty years
Herr Diedrich on the shore appears,

Looking as young, and fair and hearty,
As when he joined the ocean party;
And so well dressed he ne'er was seen,
In coat and small clothes, bottle green.
He seemed to have a mine of "chink,"
He stood old neighbors all they'd drink.
But never once went near the door,
He left so many years before.
For old Frau Smitzerl was, they told him,
Still hale and hearty, and might—scold him.

That night again he disappears,
And for another twenty years
Dame Smitzerl got along without him;
The neighbors they forgot about him,

Then suddenly again was seen,
Dierck and his shining suit of green.
He seemed still rich, and young and spry.
He found his neighbors old and—dry.

One eve, a crony as they sat
Over their lager for a chat,
Ventured to ask of Smitzerl where
He kept himself when he wasn't *there*.
At this, Von Smitzerl slyly winked,
A score of yellow ducats chinked,
Then to this wondering friend related,
The story that is here narrated.
And furthermore, gave him a notion,

Of high old times beneath the ocean.
Of emerald bowers, and coral beds,
Of mermaid blondes with pea green heads,
Of countless treasure, diamond mines,
Limburger cheese and Hamburg wines,
And bags of things that in the sea,
They had at hand full lavishly.
"His mer-wife was no scold," he said,
"No cabbage patch was to be wed;
No tubs of water had to bring.
On washdays from a distant spring,
No wood to chop, no fires to light.
But just loaf round from morn 'till night,
With jolly comrades, half seas over,
And live in luxury and clover.
And more, we ne'er grow old nor crusty,
But in the salt keep fresh and lusty."
"He had no wish," he said, "to stay
Long from his ocean home away.
Earth was so dull, and slow, and grim,
One day on shore sufficed for him."
He only came for this one reason,
To see Mc Cue's Hats in their season.

Mc Cue Bros., Hatters, 92 Broadway

PART III

1900–1950

Coney Island
1911

Why did you bring me here?
The sand is white with snow,
Over the wooden domes
The winter sea-winds blow—
There is no shelter near,
    Come, let us go.

With foam of icy lace
The sea creeps up the sand,
The wind is like a hand
That strikes us in the face.
Doors that June set a-swing
Are bolted long ago;
We try them uselessly—
Alas, there cannot be
For us a second spring;
    Come, let us go.

Our Camilla

1916

Today we had a funeral for Camilla,
All along Spring Street past the candy-store.
The street looks different when you're in a carriage,
You notice things you never saw before,
And feel so strange—
And all the other children stop and stare.
I used to stare, too, once, and want to ride—
I wore my new black coat, and mama cried.
The day it snowed Camilla had no carfare,
We never had a horse until today:
We had two for Camilla, trimmed with jet;
We left her out in Brooklyn—
She ain't home yet.

CHARLES REZNIKOFF

from Rhythms, 7
1918

On Brooklyn Bridge I saw a man drop dead.
It meant no more than if he were a sparrow.

Above us rose Manhattan;
below, the river spread to meet sea and sky.

Brooklyn Bridge
1925

Coolidge, cut loose
a joyful shout!
For something good
    I won't scrimp on words.
Blush from
    praise,
        like our homeland's red flag,
even though you're
    the un-united states
            of
America.

As a crazed believer
        goes into
                a church,
or retreats
    to a plain, austere
                hermitage cell,
so I
    in the evening's
                graying haze,
step out,
    humble, onto Brooklyn Bridge.
As a conqueror
    makes his way into a
                broken city,
on cannons with muzzles
    as tall as giraffes—
so I, drunk with glory,
        hungry for life,
climb up,
    proud,
        onto Brooklyn Bridge.

As a foolish artist
            presses his gaze
keen and tender,
        onto a museum Madonna,
so I,
    tossed to the stars,
                    look down
from the skies
    at New York
            through Brooklyn Bridge.
New York,
    stifling and oppressive
                        'til evening,
has forgotten
    its strained height
                    and what pains it,
and only
            house spirits
arise
        in its windows' clear glow.
Here
    the itch of the elevated
        is hardly a bother.
And only
    by this
        little itch
do you realize:
    trains
        are crawling by with a rattle,
like dishes
            being stacked in a sideboard.
And while
    a shop-keeper
hauls sugar
        from a factory that seems to rise
                        from the river's edge,
the masts
    passing under the bridge
are no more
        than pin-size.

I'm proud
      of this
              steel mile,
in which
      my visions have come to life—
the fight
   for construction
               instead of style,
rigorous calculation
     of bolts
            and steel.
And if
   the end
      of the world arrives—
chaos
     smashes
        the planet to bits
and the only
      thing left is
             this
bridge rearing up from the dust of destruction,
then,
   just as prehistoric reptiles
             standing in museums
regain their flesh
      from bones thinner
             than needles,
so
   with this bridge,
      the geologist of the centuries
would be able
     to recreate
            the present days.
He will say:
   And this
        steel paw
united
      seas and prairies,

from here
   Europe
         burst westward,
scattering
   Indian feathers
         on the wind.
This rib here
   resembles
     a machine.
Imagine:
   after placing
a steel leg
   on Manhattan,
      could there be enough hands,
to pull Brooklyn
   up to yourself
     by the lip?
By the strands
   of electrical wires
I know—
   it's the
        post-steam age,
here
   people
     have already
        ranted on the radio,
here
   people
     have already
        soared up in planes.
Here
   life
     was
        carefree—for some,
for others —
   a hungry
        drawn-out wail.
From here
   the unemployed

threw themselves
    head first
        into the Hudson.*

And further
    my picture
        continues unhindered
on cables strung up
    to the feet of the stars.
I see—
    here
        stood Mayakovsky,
stood
    and built verse, one word at a time,
I look,
    as an Eskimo stares at a train,
my eyes fix
    as a tick fixes onto an ear.
Brooklyn Bridge—
yes . . .
    quite a thing here!

* Mayakovsky mistakes the East River for the Hudson.

Proem: To Brooklyn Bridge
1930

How many dawns, chill from his rippling rest
The seagull's wings shall dip and pivot him,
Shedding white rings of tumult, building high
Over the chained bay waters Liberty—

Then, with inviolate curve, forsake our eyes
As apparitional as sails that cross
Some page of figures to be filed away;
—Till elevators drop us from our day . . .

I think of cinemas, panoramic sleights
With multitudes bent toward some flashing scene
Never disclosed, but hastened to again,
Foretold to other eyes on the same screen;

And Thee, across the harbor, silver-paced
As though the sun took step of thee, yet left
Some motion ever unspent in thy stride,—
Implicitly thy freedom staying thee!

Out of some subway scuttle, cell or loft
A bedlamite speeds to thy parapets,
Tilting there momently, shrill shirt ballooning,
A jest falls from the speechless caravan.

Down Wall, from girder into street noon leaks,
A rip-tooth of the sky's acetylene;
All afternoon the cloud-flown derricks turn . . .
Thy cables breathe the North Atlantic still.

And obscure as that heaven of the Jews,
Thy guerdon . . . Accolade thou dost bestow
Of anonymity time cannot raise:
Vibrant reprieve and pardon thou dost show.

O harp and altar, of the fury fused,
(How could mere toil align thy choiring strings!)
Terrific threshold of the prophet's pledge,
Prayer of pariah, and the lover's cry,—

Again the traffic lights that skim thy swift
Unfractioned idiom, immaculate sigh of stars,
Beading thy path—condense eternity:
And we have seen night lifted in thine arms.

Under thy shadow by the piers I waited;
Only in darkness is thy shadow clear.
The City's fiery parcels all undone,
Already snow submerges an iron year . . .

O Sleepless as the river under thee,
Vaulting the sea, the prairies' dreaming sod,
Unto us lowliest sometime sweep, descend
And of the curveship lend a myth to God.

I Am . . .

1932

I am Mani Leyb, whose name is sung—
In Brownsville, Yehupets, and farther, they know it:
Among cobblers, a splendid cobbler; among
Poetical circles, a splendid poet.

A boy straining over the cobbler's last
On moonlit nights . . . like a command,
Some hymn struck at my heart, and fast
The awl fell from my trembling hand.

Gracious, the first Muse came to meet
The cobbler with a kiss, and, young,
I tasted the Word that comes in a sweet
Shuddering first to the speechless tongue.

And my tongue flowed like a limpid stream,
My song rose as from some other place;
My world's doors opened onto dream;
My labor, my bread, were sweet with grace.

And all of the others, the shoemaker boys,
Thought that my singing was simply grand:
For their bitter hearts, my poems were joys.
Their source? They could never understand.

For despair in their working day's vacuity
They mocked me, spat at me a good deal,
And gave me the title, in perpetuity,
Of Purple Patchmaker, Poet and Heel.

Farewell then, brothers, I must depart:
Your cobbler's bench is not for me.
With songs in my breast, the Muse in my heart,
I went among poets, a poet to be.

When I came, then, among their company,
Newly fledged from out my shell,
They lauded and they laureled me,
Making me one of their number as well.

O Poets, inspired and pale, and free
As all the winged singers of the air,
We sang of beauties wild to see
Like happy beggars at a fair.

We sang, and the echoing world resounded.
From pole to pole chained hearts were hurled,
While we gagged on hunger, our sick chest pounded:
More than one of us left this world.

And God, who feedeth even the worm—
Was not quite lavish with his grace,
So I crept back, threadbare and infirm,
To sweat for bread at my working place.

But blessed be, Muse, for your bounties still,
Though your granaries will yield no bread—
At my bench, with a pure and lasting will,
I'll serve you solely until I am dead.

In Brownsville, Yehupets, beyond them, even,
My name shall ever be known, O Muse.
And I'm not a cobbler who writes, thank heaven,
But a poet who makes shoes.

DELMORE SCHWARTZ

The Ballad of the Children of the Czar
1938

1

The children of the Czar
Played with a bouncing ball

In the May morning, in the Czar's garden,
Tossing it back and forth.

It fell among the flowerbeds
Or fled to the north gate.

A daylight moon hung up
In the Western sky, bald white.

Like Papa's face, said Sister,
Hurling the white ball forth.

2

While I ate a baked potato
Six thousand miles apart,

In Brooklyn, in 1916,
Aged two, irrational.

When Franklin D. Roosevelt
Was an Arrow Collar ad.

O Nicholas! Alas! Alas!
My grandfather coughed in your army,

Hid in a wine-stinking barrel,
For three days in Bucharest

Then left for America
To become a king himself.

3

I am my father's father,
You are your children's guilt.

In history's pity and terror
The child is Aeneas again;

Troy is in the nursery,
The rocking horse is on fire.

Child labor! The child must carry
His fathers on his back.

But seeing that so much is past
And that history has no ruth

For the individual,
Who drinks tea, who catches cold,

Let anger be general:
I hate an abstract thing.

4

Brother and sister bounced
The bounding, unbroken ball,

The shattering sun fell down
Like swords upon their play,

Moving eastward among the stars
Toward February and October.

But the Maywind brushed their cheeks
Like a mother watching sleep,

And if for a moment they fight
Over the bouncing ball

And sister pinches brother
And brother kicks her shins,

Well! The heart of man is known:
It is a cactus bloom.

5

The ground on which the ball bounces
Is another bouncing ball.

The wheeling, whirling world
Makes no will glad.

Spinning in its spotlight darkness,
It is too big for their hands.

A pitiless, purposeless Thing,
Arbitrary and unspent,

Made for no play, for no children,
But chasing only itself.

The innocent are overtaken,
They are not innocent.

They are their father's fathers,
The past is inevitable.

6

Now, in another October
Of this tragic star,

I see my second year,
I eat my baked potato.

It is my buttered world,
But, poked by my unlearned hand,

It falls from the highchair down
And I begin to howl.

And I see the ball roll under
The iron gate which is locked.

Sister is screaming, brother is howling,
The ball has evaded their will.

Even a bouncing ball
Is uncontrollable,

And is under the garden wall.
I am overtaken by terror

Thinking of my father's fathers,
And of my own will.

Sleepless City (Brooklyn Bridge Nocturne)

1940

Out in the sky, no one sleeps. No one, no one.
No one sleeps.
Lunar creatures sniff and circle the dwellings.
Live iguanas will come to bite the men who don't dream,
and the brokenhearted fugitive will meet on street corners
an incredible crocodile resting beneath the tender protest of the
      stars.

Out in the world, no one sleeps. No one, no one.
No one sleeps.
There is a corpse in the farthest graveyard
complaining for three years
because of an arid landscape in his knee;
and a boy who was buried this morning cried so much
they had to call the dogs to quiet him.

Life is no dream. Watch out! Watch out! Watch out!
We fall down stairs and eat the moist earth,
or we climb to the snow's edge with the choir of dead dahlias.
But there is no oblivion, no dream:
raw flesh. Kisses tie mouths
in a tangle of new veins
and those who are hurt will hurt without rest
and those who are frightened by death will carry it on their
      shoulders.

One day
horses will live in the taverns
and furious ants
will attack the yellow skies that take refuge in the eyes of cattle.
Another day
we'll witness the resurrection of dead butterflies,
and still walking in a landscape of gray sponges and silent ships,
we'll see our ring shine and rose spill from our tongues.

Watch out! Watch out! Watch out!

Those still marked by claws and cloudburst,
that boy who cries because he doesn't know about the invention
     of bridges,
or that corpse that has nothing more than its head and one
     shoe—
they all must be led to the wall where iguanas and serpents wait,
where the bear's teeth wait,
where the mummified hand of a child waits
and the camel's fur bristles with a violent blue chill.

Out in the sky, no one sleeps. No one, no one.
No one sleeps.
But if someone closes his eyes,
whip him, my children, whip him!
Let there be a panorama of open eyes
and bitter inflamed wounds.
Out in the world, no one sleeps. No one. No one.
I've said it before.
No one sleeps.
But at night, if someone has too much moss on his temples,
open the trap doors so he can see in moonlight
the fake goblets, the venom, and the skull of the theaters.

CHARLES REZNIKOFF

CHARLES REZNIKOFF

Get the Gasworks
1948

Get the gasworks into a poem,
and you've got the smoke and smokestacks,
the mottled red and yellow tenements,
and grimy kids who curse with the pungency
of the odor of gas. You've got America, boy.

Sketch in the river and barges,
all dirty and slimy.
How do the seagulls stay so white?
And always cawing like little mad geniuses?
You've got the kind of living
that makes the kind of thinking we do:
gaswork smokestack whistle tooting wisecracks.
They don't come because we like it that way,
but because we find it outside our window each morning,
in soot on the furniture,
and trucks carrying coal for gas,
the kid hot after the ball under the wheel.
He gets it over the belly, all right.
He dies there.

So the kids keep tossing the ball around
after the funeral.
So the cops keep chasing them,
so the mamas keep hollering,
and papa flings his newspaper outward,
in disgust with discipline.

PART IV

1950s

Salt Water Taffy

1954

Their long skirts stiffened by the salty air
Waved at the sea's edge to those bathing;
High cries drowned out the ocean's roar
When, accidentally, they went wading.

The sweet sun sieved summer afternoons.
The beach was a waste of lace, and sandy.
Raspberry sherbet went down in spoons
To prove the summer was a box of candy.

The boardwalk, tigered, sun by shadow,
Whirled them across its thin bars daily;
Bracken and seaweed, but no meadow;
Veered with the wind, wailing palely.

Noons, under strict shade, sad they sat,
Wishing the day's loose sails would tighten;
Taffy was all they doted on, yet
Love might come at Coney, Brighton.

Where are they now, those hour-glass girls
Who walked the boards at Atlantic City
Eating their sticks of salt-water taffy,
To whom the summer was a box of candy?

It Happened on the Fourth Avenue Local, Brooklyn, On My 77th Birthday, March 20, 1955

1955

"Wake up!" the subway guard exclaimed
    In no uncertain voice,
"For this is Seventy-seven' Street,
    And you are Mister Royce."
"Thanks for your solicitude,"
    I said, "but if I'm still alive,
I will remain upon the train
    'Til I reach Ninety-five."

Invitation to Miss Marianne Moore
1955

From Brooklyn, over the Brooklyn Bridge, on this fine morning,
   please come flying.
In a cloud of fiery pale chemicals,
   please come flying,
to the rapid rolling of thousands of small blue drums
descending out of the mackcrcl sky
over the glittering grandstand of harbor-water,
   please come flying.

Whistles, pennants and smoke are blowing. The ships
are signaling cordially with multitudes of flags
rising and falling like birds all over the harbor.
Enter: two rivers, gracefully bearing
countless little pellucid jellies
in cut-glass epergnes dragging with silver chains.
The flight is safe; the weather is all arranged.
The waves are running in verses this fine morning.
   Please come flying.

Come with the pointed toe of each black shoe
trailing a sapphire highlight,
with a black capeful of butterfly wings and bon-mots,
with heaven knows how many angels all riding
on the broad black brim of your hat,
   please come flying.

Bearing a musical inaudible abacus,
a slight censorious frown, and blue ribbons,
   please come flying.
Facts and skyscrapers glint in the tide; Manhattan
is all awash with morals this fine morning,
   so please come flying.

Mounting the sky with natural heroism,
above the accidents, above the malignant movies,

the taxicabs and injustices at large,
while horns are resounding in your beautiful ears
that simultaneously listen to
a soft uninvented music, fit for the musk deer,
 please come flying.

For whom the grim museums will behave
like courteous male bower-birds,
for whom the agreeable lions lie in wait
on the steps of the Public Library,
eager to rise and follow through the doors
up into the reading rooms,
 please come flying.
We can sit down and weep; we can go shopping,
or play at a game of constantly being wrong
with a priceless set of vocabularies,
or we can bravely deplore, but please
 please come flying.

With dynasties of negative constructions
darkening and dying around you,
with grammar that suddenly turns and shines
like flocks of sandpipers flying,
 please come flying.

Come like a light in the white mackerel sky,
come like a daytime comet
with a long unnebulous train of words,
from Brooklyn, over the Brooklyn Bridge, on this fine morning,
 please come flying.

24
1958

We squat upon the beach of love
   among Picasso mandolins struck full of sand
      and buried catspaws that know no sphinx
        and picnic papers
          dead crabs' claws
            and starfish prints

We squat upon the beach of love
   among the beached mermaids
      with their bawling babies and bald husbands
        and homemade wooden animals
          with icecream spoons for feet
            which cannot walk or love
              except to eat

We squat upon the brink of love
   and are secure as only squatters are
      among the puddled leavings
          of salt sex's tides
     and the sweet semen rivulets
      and limp buried peckers
   in the sand's soft flesh

And still we laugh
   and still we run
      and still we throw ourselves
         upon love's boats
      but it is deeper
       and much later
            than we think
    and all goes down
      and all our love buoys fail us

And we drink and drown

Hometown Piece for Messrs. Alston And Reese
1959

> *To the tune: "Li'l baby, don't say a word: Mama goin' to buy you a mocking-bird.*
> *Bird don't sing: Mama goin' to sell it and buy a brass ring."*

"Millennium," yes; "pandemonium"!
Roy Campanella leaps high. Dodgerdom

crowned, had Johnny Podres on the mound.
Buzzie Bavasi and the Press gave ground;

the team slapped, mauled, and asked the Yankees' match,
"How did you feel when Sandy Amoros made the catch?"

"I said to myself"—pitcher for all innings—
"as I walked back to the mound I said, 'Everything's

getting better and better.'" (Zest: they've zest.
"Hope springs eternal in the Brooklyn breast."

And would the Dodger Band in 8, row I, relax
if they saw the collector of income tax?

Ready with a tune if that should occur:
"Why Not Take All of Me—All of Me, Sir?")

Another series. Round-tripper Duke at bat,
"Four hundred feet from home plate"; more like that.

A neat bunt, please; a cloud-breaker, a drive
like Jim Gilliam's great big one. Hope's alive.

Homered, flied out, fouled? Our "stylish stout"
so nimble Campanella will have him out.

A-squat in double-headers four hundred times a day,
he says that in a measure the pleasure is the pay:

catcher to pitcher, a nice easy throw
almost as if he'd just told it to go.

Willie Mays should be a Dodger. He should—
a lad for Roger Craig and Clem Labine to elude;

but you have an omen, pennant-winning Peewee,
on which we are looking superstitiously.

Ralph Branca has Preacher Roe's number; recall?
and there's Don Bessent; he can really fire the ball.

As for Gil Hodges, in custody of first—
"He'll do it by himself." Now a specialist—versed

in an extension reach far into the box seats—
he lengthens up, leans and gloves the ball. He defeats

expectation by a whisker. The modest star,
irked by one misplay, is no hero by a hair;

in a strikeout slaughter when what could matter more,
he lines a homer to the signboard and has changed the score.

Then for his nineteenth season, a home run—
with four of six runs batted in—Carl Furillo's the big gun;

almost dehorned the foe—has fans dancing in delight.
Jake Pitler and his Playground "get a Night"—

Jake, that hearty man, made heartier by a harrier
who can bat as well as field—Don Demeter.

Shutting them out for nine innings—hitter too—
Carl Erskine leaves Cimoli nothing to do.

Take off the goat-horns, Dodgers, that egret
which two very fine base-stealers can offset.

You've got plenty: Jackie Robinson
and Campy and big Newk, and Dodgerdom again
watching everything you do. You won last year. Come on.

PART V

1960s

National Cold Storage Company
1960

The National Cold Storage company contains
More things than you can dream of.
Hard by the Brooklyn Bridge it stands
In a litter of freight cars,
Tugs to one side; the other, the traffic
Of the Long Island Expressway.
I myself have dropped into it in seven years
Midnight tossings, plans for escape, the shakes.
Add this to the national total—
Grant's tomb, the Civil War, Arlington,
The young President dead.
Above the warehouse and beneath the stars
The poets creep on the harp of the Bridge.
But see,
They fall into the National Cold Storage Company
One by one. The wind off the river is too cold,
Or the times too rough, or the Bridge
Is not a harp at all. Or maybe
A monstrous birth inside the warehouse
Must be fed by everything—ships, poems,
Stars, all the years of our lives.

Ave Maria
1960

Mothers of America
    let your kids go to the movies!
get them out of the house so they won't know what you're up to
it's true that fresh air is good for the body
       but what about the soul
that grows in darkness, embossed by silvery images
and when you grow old as grow old you must
         they won't hate you
they won't criticise you they won't know
    they'll be in some glamorous country
they first saw on a Saturday afternoon or playing hookey

they may even be grateful to you
       for their first sexual experience
which only cost you a quarter
    and didn't upset the peaceful home
they will know where candy bars come from
       and gratuitous bags of popcorn
as gratuitous as leaving the movie before it's over
with a pleasant stranger whose apartment is in the
         Heaven on Earth Bldg
near the Williamsburg Bridge
    oh mothers you will have made the little tykes
so happy because if nobody does pick them up in the movies
they won't know the difference
       and if somebody does it'll be sheer gravy
and they'll have been truly entertained either way
instead of hanging around the yard
       or up in their room
         hating you
prematurely since you won't have done anything horribly mean
except keeping them from the darker joys
       it's unforgivable the latter

so don't blame me if you won't take this advice
        and the family breaks up

so don't blame me if you won't take this advice
        and the family breaks up

███

so don't blame me if you won't take this advice
        and the family breaks up
and your children grow old and blind in front of a TV set
                             seeing
movies you wouldn't let them see when they were young

63

The Bridge

(For wieners & mcclure)

1961

I have forgotten the head
of where I am. Here at the bridge. 2
bars, down the street, seeming
to wrap themselves around my fingers, the day,
screams in me; pitiful like a little girl
you sense will be dead before the winter
is over.

I can't see the bridge now, I've past
it, its shadow, we drove through, headed out
along the cold insensitive roads to what
we wanted to call "ourselves."
"How does the bridge go?" Even tho
you find yourself in its length
strung out along its breadth, waiting
for the cold sun to tear out your eyes. Enamoured
of its blues, spread out in the silk clubs of
this autumn tune. The changes are difficult, when
you hear them, & know they are all in you, the chords

of your disorder meddle with your would be disguises.
Sifting in, down, upon your head, with the sun & the insects.

(Late feeling) Way down till it barely, after that rush of
wind & odor reflected from hills you have forgotten the color
when you touch the water, & it closes, slowly, around your head.

The bridge will be behind you, that music you know, that place,
you feel when you look up to say, it is me, & I have forgotten,

all the things, you told me to love, to try to understand, the
bridge will stand, high up in the clouds & the light & you,

(when you have let the song run out) will be sliding through
unmentionable black.

It is Sticky in the Subway
1961

How I love this girl who until
This minute, I never knew existed on
The face of this earth.

      I sit opposite
Her, thinking myself as stupid as that
Photograph, maudlin in Mumford, of
Orpheus.

    A kinkled adolescent
Defies the Authorities by
Smoking a butt right next to me. He is
Of Romeos the least attractive who
Has played the role.

      He
Smirks, squints, glues his eyes to her
Tightly entethered teeth, scratches
His moist passion on some scratch paper.

     Her eyes
Accuse Plato of non-en
Tity. Most delightful creature of moment's
              above-ground.

The Men of Sheepshead
1962

Eric—we used to call him Eric—
And Charlie Weber: I knew them well,
Men of another century. And still at Sheepshead
If a man carries pliers
Or maul down these rambling piers he is a man who fetches
Power into the afternoon
                Speaking of things

End-for-end, butted to each other,
Dove-tailed, tenoned, doweled—Who is not at home
Among these men? who make a home
Of half truth, rules of thumb
Of cam and lever and whose docks and piers
Extend into the sea so self-contained.

A Letter From Brooklyn

1962

An old lady writes me in a spidery style,
Each character trembling, and I see a veined hand
Pellucid as paper, traveling on a skein
Of such frail thoughts its thread is often broken;
Or else the filament from which a phrase is hung
Dims to my sense, but caught, it shines like steel,
As touch a line, and the whole web will feel.
She describes my father, yet I forget her face
More easily than my father's yearly dying;
Of her I remember small, buttoned boots and the place
She kept in our wooden church on those Sundays
Whenever her strength allowed;
Grey haired, thin voice, perpetually bowed.

"I am Mable Rawlins," she writes, "and know both your parents";
He is dead, Miss Rawlins, but God bless your tense:
"Your father was a dutiful, honest,
Faithful and useful person."
For such plain praise what fame is recompense?
"A horn-painter, he painted delicately on horn,
He used to sit around the table and paint pictures."
The peace of God needs nothing to adorn
It, nor glory nor ambition.
"He is twenty-eight years buried," she writes, "he was called
        home,
And is, I am sure, doing greater work."

The strength of one frail hand in a dim room
Somewhere in Brooklyn, patient and assured,
Restores my sacred duty to the Word.
"Home, home," she can write, with such short time to live,
Alone as she spins the blessings of her years;
Not withered of beauty if she can bring such tears,
Nor withdrawn from the world that breaks its lovers so;

Heaven is to her the place where painters go,
All who bring beauty on frail shell or horn,
There was all made, thence their lux-mundi drawn,
Drawn, drawn, till the thread is resilient steel,
Lost though it seems in the darkening periods,
And there they return to do work that is God's.
So this old lady writes, and again I believe.
I believe it all, and for no man's death I grieve.

Street
1965

Ah these are the poor,
These are the poor—

Bergen street.

Humiliation,
Hardship . . .

Nor are they very good to each other;
It is not that. I want

An end of poverty
As much as anyone

For the sake of intelligence,
'The conquest of existence'—

It has been said, and is true—

And this is real pain,
Moreover. It is terrible to see the children,

The righteous little girls;
So good, they expect to be so good . . .

TONY TOWLE

The Allegorical Figure of Brooklyn
1966

The Allegorical Figure of Brooklyn is right here,
there where you're standing, and here's how it works.
The lamps go on and we walk through miles of parks;
the rain and the sleet are brought on, we travel
to Queens for two weeks of vacation; the sun returns
and the grass and farms, the villages of Brooklyn
continue to grow, and the spacious terrace and
oily sand of Brooklyn breathe, to be rocked slowly
by the Figure, and back toward home on the BMT
we smile at the tender Figure and wave goodbye.

Personal Poem #9
1969

It's 8:54 a.m. in Brooklyn it's the 26th of July
and it's probably 8:54 in Manhattan but I'm
in Brooklyn I'm eating English muffins and drinking
Pepsi and I'm thinking of how Brooklyn is New
York City too how odd I usually think of it
as something all its own like Bellows Falls like
Little Chute like Uijongbu
                              I never thought
on the Williamsburg Bridge I'd come so much to Brooklyn
just to see lawyers and cops who don't even carry guns
taking my wife away and bringing her back
                                 No
and I never thought Dick would be back at Gude's
beard shaved off long hair cut and Carol reading
his books when we were playing cribbage and watching
the sun come up over the Navy Yard a-
cross the river
                     I think I was thinking
when I was ahead I'd be somewhere like Perry Street
erudite dazzling slim and badly-loved
contemplating my new book of poetry
to be printed in simple type on old brown paper
feminine marvelous and tough

Similes

1969

Indifferent as a statue
to the slogan
scribbled on its pedestal.

The way an express train
snubs the passengers at a local station.

Like a notebook forgotten on the seat in the 'bus,
full of names, addresses and telephone numbers:
important, no doubt, to the owner—
and of no interest whatever
to anyone else.

Words like drops of water on a stove—
a hiss and gone.

[110]

1969

The man who planned the bridge
had his foot crushed between the piling and the dock
by a ferryboat. That was useless, ferryboat!
He died
but the ferryboats, too, are gone.

PART VI

1970s

Hutch Waters
Harvey Shapiro
Gabriel Preil
Robert Lowell
Muriel Rukeyser
Audre Lorde
June Jordan
Diane di Prima
Irving Feldman
Enid Dame
Charles Martin
Maurice Kenny

Unpaid Bills (From *Africa in Brooklyn*)
1971

. . . . and the white man said,

"Mr. Black man, why is it that so
many Negras don' pay their bills?"

. . . . and the
black man said,

"You see, Mr. White man, it's like
this. Suppose you were sittin' home
one night watchin' T.V. an' there
was a knock on the door an' when you
opened the door there stood a big
Black man an' he said,

    'PARDON ME, MISTER
    WHITE MAN, BUT I
    CAME TO COLLECT MY
    FORTY ACRES AND MY
    MULE.'?"

The Synagogue on Kane Street

1971

Anachronisms are pleasant.
I like shifting periods
As the young rabbi doesn't shift tones
Saying "The Ethics of Maimonides"
And "The Reader's Digest."

There is no reason for survival.
As we drift outward
The tribal gods wave farewell.

It is the mother synagogue of Brooklyn.
We are a handful in the cathedral.

When I was asked
I said the blessing
For the reading of the scroll
Almost correctly.

The reader had a silver pointer.

The parchment before me
Was like a beginning.

Moving
1972 (Hebrew), 1985 (English)

In my old neighborhood the finest Hasidim
made bridges of the street.
Henry Miller, on the other hand,
invented for himself a vagabond.
I, in that same place,
bore on my shoulder
birds of Hebrew song,
while ships departed for one sea or another.

Now my new, my seething neighborhood
seems glad to make me old,
even though Hcine blossoms here
from clouded marble,
and another poet keeps saying
that only God makes trees.

Both are younger than a morning smile,
but even one as tired of banalities as I am
accepts unquestioningly that banal observation:
no one can make time green.

In the Forties 3
1973

By August, Brooklyn turned autumn, all
Prospect Park could mirror. No sound; no talk;
dead matches nicked the water and expired
in target-circles of inverted sky,
nature's looking-glass . . . a little cold!
Our day was cold and short, love, and its sun
numb as the red carp, twenty inches long,
panting, a weak old dog, below a smashed
oar floating from the musty dock. . . . The fish
is fungus now; I wear a swollen face. . . .
I rowed for our reflection, but it slid
between my hands aground. There the squirrel,
a conservative and vegetarian,
keeps his roots and freehold, Love, unsliding.

Coney Island, from *Houdini*
1973

Coney Island, Coney Island,
No need to let me know,
No need to tell me so
I need you now to show me . . .

Some. Show me what's under the counter,
       Show me what's under your skin,
       Show me the way to get out
       And I'll show you the way to get in.

Others. Show me life, show me lives, people in dives,
        Show me yells, show me smells, and grimy hotels,
        Clams, yams, lobster and shrimps,
        Sand, candy, panders and pimps,
        Show me bim, show me bam, bamboozle me,
        Booze me and use me and foozle me,
        Show me rides, show me slides, people in tides,
        Show me money, show me funny, show me the sea,
                        You, show, me.

Houdini and Beatrice. Let me see,
                       Let me feel,
                       Let me know what is real,
                       Let me bel-
                              ieve.

Cables to Rage
Or
I've Been Talking on This Street Corner
a Hell of a Long Time
1974

This is how I came to be loved
by loving myself loveless.

One day I slipped in the snowy gutter of Brighton Beach
and the booted feet passing
me by on the curb squished my laundry ticket
into the slush and I thought oh fuck it now
I'll never get my clean sheet and cried bitter tears
into the snow under my cheek in that gutter in Brighton Beach
Brooklyn where I was living because it was cheap

In a furnished room with cooking privileges
and there was an old thrown-away mama who lived down the hall
a yente who sat all day long in our common kitchen
weeping because her children made her live with a schwartze
and while she wept she drank up all my Cream Soda
every day before I came home.
Then she sat and watched me watching my chicken feet stewing
on the Fridays when I got paid
and she taught me to boil old corn in the husk
to make it taste green and fresh.
There were not many pleasures in that winter
and I loved Cream Soda
there were not many people in that winter
and I came to hate that old woman.
The winter I got fat on stale corn on the cob
and chicken foot stew and the day before Christmas
having no presents to wrap
I poured two ounces of Nux Vomica into a bottle of Cream Soda
and listened to the old lady puke all night long.

When spring came I crossed the river again
moving up in the world six and half stories
and one day on the corner of eighth street across from Wana-
    makers
which had burned down while I was away in Brooklyn—
where I caught the bus for work every day
a bus driver slowed down at the bus stop one morning—
I was late it was raining and my jacket was soaked—
and then speeded past without stopping when he saw my face.

I have been given other doses of truth—
that particular form of annihilation—
shot through by the cold eye of the way things are baby
and left for dead on a hundred streets of this city
but oh that captain marvel glance
brushing up against my skull like a steel bar
in passing
and my heart withered sheets in the gutter
passing passing
booted feet and bus drivers
and old yentes in Brighton Beach kitchens
SHIT! said the king and the whole court strained
passing
me out as an ill-tempered wind
lashing around the corner
of 125th Street and Lenox.

(For Michael Angelo Thompson)
1975

(October 25, 1959 – March 23, 1973)

So Brooklyn has become a holy place

The streets have turned to meadowland
where
wild
free
ponies
eat among the wild
free
flowers
growing there

                              Please do not forget.
A tiger does not fall or stumble
broken by an accident.
A tiger does not lose his stride or
clumsy
slip and slide to tragedy
that buzzards feast upon.
                              Do not forget.
The Black prince Michael Black boy
our younger brother
has not "died"
he
has not "passed away"
the Black prince Michael Black boy
our younger brother
                              He was killed.
                              He did not die.
It was the city took him off
(that city bus)
and smashed him suddenly

to death
deliberate.

It was the city took him off
the hospital
that turned him down the hospital
that turned away from so much beauty
bleeding
bleeding
in Black struggle
     just to live.
It was the city took him off
the casket names and faces
of the hatred spirit
stripped the force the
laughter and the agile power
of the child

           He did not die.
           A tiger does not fall.
           Do not forget.

The streets have turned to meadowland
where
wild
free
ponies
eat among the wild
free
flowers
growing there
and Brooklyn
has become a holy place.

Backyard

1975

where angels turned into honeysuckle & poured nectar into my
    mouth
where I french-kissed the roses in the rain
where demons tossed me a knife to kill my father in the stark
    simplicity of the sky
where I never cried
where all the roofs were black
where no one opened the venetian blinds
O Brooklyn! Brooklyn!
where fences crumbled under the weight of rambling roses
and naked plaster women bent eternally white over birdbaths
the icicles on the chains of the swings tore my fingers
& the creaking tomato plants tore my heart as they wrapped their
    roots around fish heads rotting beneath them
& the phonograph too creaked Caruso come down from the skies;
    Tito Gobbi in gondola; Gigli ridiculous in soldier uniform;
    Lanza frenetic
& the needle tore at the records & my fingers
tore poems into little pieces & watched the sky
where clouds torn into pieces & livid w/ neon or rain
scudded away from Red Hook, away from Gowanus Canal, away
from Brooklyn Navy Yard where everybody worked, to fall to pieces
    over Clinton Street
and the plaster saints in the yard never looked at the naked
    women
    in the birdbaths
and the folks coming home from work in pizza parlor or furniture
    store, slamming wrought iron gates to come
    upon brownstone houses,
never looked at either: they saw that the lawns were dry
were eternally parched beneath red gloomy sunsets we viewed from
    a thousand brownstone stoops
leaning together by thousands on the same
wrought-iron banister, watching the sun impaled
on black St. Stephen's steeple

Leaping Clear
1976

> *Circumambulate the city of a dreamy Sabbath afternoon. Go from Corlears Hook to Co-*
> *enties Slip, and from thence, by Whitehall, northward. What do you see?—Posted like*
> *silent sentinels all around the town, stand thousands upon thousands of mortal men fixed in*
> *ocean reveries.*
>   HERMAN MELVILLE

1

Excrescence, excrement, earth
belched in buildings   the city
is the underworld in the world.
They wall space in or drag it down,
lock it underground in holes and subways,
fetid, blackened, choking.
                          Shriveled, small,
grimed with coal and ash, shovel in hand,
his dust-sputting putz in the other,
like death's demiurge come up to look
around, to smudge the evening air,
the old Polack janitor on Clinton Street,
turd squat in the tenement anus,
stands half-underground in darkness
of the cellar steps and propositions
passing children in a broken tongue.
Quickly, they crowd, they age, they plunge
into holes, and are set to work.

2

Encountered at estuary
end across beaches and dunes,
or opening out of the breakwater's
armlock, a last magnitude
of bay, or beyond the crazywork

of masts and rigging down a street
suddenly, the sea stuns
moving into itself, gray over
green over gray, with salt smell
and harbor smells, tar, flotsam,
fish smell, froth, its sentient
immense transparent space.

Walking in Coney Island, bicycling
in Bay Ridge on the crumbling water-level
promenade under the Verrazano,
walking the heights above the Narrows, driving
on Brooklyn Heights, then slowly at night
under the East River Drive past the empty
fish market, past Battery Park, and then
northward driving along the rotting piers,
or looking downriver from Washington Heights
into the harbor's distant opening,
I recovered one summer in New York
the magical leisure of the lost sea-space.
Breathing, I entered, I became
the open doorway to the empty marvel,
the first Atlantis of light.

Windy sun below the Narrows,
Gravesend scud and whitecaps,
coal garbage gravel
scows bucking off Bensonhurst,
Richmond blueblurred
westward, and high
into the blue
supreme clarity,
it gleams aloft, alert
at the zenith
of leaping, speed
all blown to the wind
—what, standing in air,
what does it say
looking out out out?

And the light
    (everywhere,
off ridge, rock, window, deep,
drop) says,
        I leap clear.

            3

Recalled from the labor of creation,
they were glancing as they flew, and saw
looking out to them the shimmering
of the million points of view. To see
Brooklyn so on a sabbath afternoon
from the heights, to be there beyond
the six days, the chronicle of labors,
to stand in the indestructible space,
encompass the world into whose center
you fly, and be the light looking!

The demiurge of an age of bronze
sees his handiwork and says it is good,
laying down his tools forever.
To see Brooklyn so in the spacious ease
of sabbath afternoon above the Narrows
is to say over and over what our speechless eyes
behold, that it is good, it is good, the first
Brooklyn of the senses, ardent and complete
as it was in the setting out of the sabbath.

Flatbush Incantation
1977

So this is Brooklyn!
The sad wet trees
the green nostalgic rain
the houses, gray, disheveled,
pulled out of shape,
against whose walls
the roses break,
surprising, red.

The men
wear black
and beards.
The women shawl their hair
and carry babies.
And Yiddish
is a spoken language
on Coney Island Avenue.

It's easy to become
another person, here:
a fourteen-year old girl
behind a rainy window, under
a sweetly rotting roof.
A self-declared agnostic
who bites her nails to blood
who writes intense
freeverse with small i's
who hates it all:
the house, the rain, herself
who sneaks into the Village
and catches whiffs of jazz
from smoke-black basements
who hears the workshirt boys
(from Brooklyn also)

beat Marx against their beermugs.
Who, not quite consummated,
takes the D-train home.

The windows of
the candystore—
unbarred, unbraced.
I drink a perfect eggcream
at a marble counter.
The man says, "Good? Of course.
I'm good, too. That's why
no woman ever
wanted me. I'm too good."
The Chasid on the next stool
glares unhappily.

Walking home
through the graying rain
anachronistic in
my hair-knots, my serape
perhaps I've been
sneaked into
another incarnation
before Auschwitz, before Warsaw
before the Rosenberg case
before the cold war
iced over our roots
before the nervous breakdowns
before Vietnam

time-captured
in another, safer world
with all my possibilities
intact.

Sharks at the New York Aquarium
1978

Suddenly drawn through the thick glass plate
And swimming among them, I imagine
Myself as, briefly, part of the pattern
Traced in the water as they circulate
Endlessly, obeying the few laws
That thread the needle of their simple lives:
One moment in a window of serrated knives,
Old-fashioned razors and electric saws.
And then the sudden, steep, sidewinding pass:
No sound at all. The waters turning pink,
Then rose, then red, after a long while clear.
And here I am again, outside the tank,
Uneasily wrapped in our atmosphere!
Children almost never tap on the glass.

Dead Morning in Brooklyn Heights
1979

Had Verrazano spent rainy mornings
Drinking mugs of herbal tea
A bridge wouldn't have been built!
    There were at least a hundred occupations:
    A half-read Wolfe open on the desk,
    Shoes to polish, a sink of dinner dishes.

Washington would have never held the Heights.
Had he given into cold day-dreams;
Whitman would still be riding the Brooklyn Ferry.

    Time is not money . . . a current expression . . .
    It is the throttle of all arteries,
    The flower and fruit of all trees.

    It is a poor man who coins his morning light
    To stare down plants greening on windowsills;
    Gawk at office boys, tellers, waiters.

Every morning Norman Mailer tramps down Clark St.
To the subway at the St. George Hotel to office.
His secretaries do not write his novels.

    Even pimps ply their trade in the street below;
    Pigeons bloom on crumbs in the gutters,
    And the dead have labored at dying.

Grand Army Plaza
1980

For Ethelbert, 1977—1980

Why would anybody build a monument to civil war?

The tall man and myself tonight
we will not sleep together
we may not
either one of us
sleep
in any case
the differential between friend and lover
is a problem
definitions curse
as *nowadays we're friends*
or
we were lovers once
while
overarching the fastidious the starlit
dust
that softens space between us
is the history that bleeds
alike

the stain of skin on stone

But on this hard ground curved by memories
of union and disunion and of brothers dead
by the familiar hand
how do we face to face a man
a woman
interpenetrated
free

and reaching still toward the kiss that will
not suffocate?

We are not survivors of a civil war

We survive our love
because we go on

loving

ROBERT HERSHON

The Jurors
1980

V. the jurors respond to their wonderful names

the clerk calls out the wonderful names

anthony provenzano oreste bafi
samuel gebhardt angelo lo conti
nolan purefoy howard corrigan
lester perelman benedict rizzo

and with the calling of each name
a man rises and steps forward
because it is his name
his own magic name

he will go where he is told to go
just call him by his name

VI. the jurors discuss the high cost of living

this country's really headed for trouble, believe me
    a revolution or something
jeez, the other night i paid
    three fifty for a shrimp cocktail

yeah, and the cost of meat
you could buy an apartment house
    anyway, all the hormones they're putting in
we're all gonna be fags

VII. the jurors consider it an open and shut case

why would a cop lie
why aren't there any ashtrays in here

where do they take us for lunch
could i bum one of your cigarettes
what do you figure these clerks make
why would a cop lie

JOAN LARKIN

Housework

1982

Through this window, thin rivers
glaze a steep roof. Rain; a church of rain,
a sky—opaque pearl,
branches gemmed with rain,
houses made of rain.

I am in the kitchen
killing flies against the cabinets
with a rolled-up magazine,
no Buddhist—
I live by insisting on my hatreds.

I hate these flies.
With a restless wounding buzz
they settle on the fruit,
the wall—again, again
invading my house of rain.

Their feelers, like hard black hairs,
test the air, or my gaze.
I find I am praying
Stand still for me.
I'll devil the life out of you.

The human swarm comes in
with wet leaves on their sticky boots.
They settle on me with their needs; I am not nice.
Outside, headlights of dark cars are winding the street.
The mirror over the sink will do me in.

At five o'clock, rain done with, in darkness
the houses gather. In the livingrooms
Batman bluely flickers; the children all shut up,
All but an angry baby or a husband.
The suburb is wreathed in wet leaves.

I forget what I wanted. Was it old music
laying gold-leaf on the evening?
lamplight sweetening the carpet
like honey from Crete? a dream of/door to Egypt?
Something to do with the life force.

December turns the sky to metal,
the leaves to gutter-paper.
Leak stopped, the bedroom ceiling starts to dry.
Its skin of paint is split and curling downward.
There is a fly in this house that will not die.

C. K. WILLIAMS

The Regulars
1983

In the Colonial Luncheonette on Sixth Street they know every-
  thing there is to know, the shits.
Sam Terminadi will tell you how to gamble yourself at age sixty
  from accountant to bookie,
and Sam Finkel will tell you more than anyone cares to hear how
  to parlay an ulcer into a pension
so you can sit here drinking this shit coffee and eating these
  overfried shit eggs
while you explain that the reasons the people across the street are
  going to go bust
in the toy store they're redoing the old fish market into—the fa-
  ther and son plastering,
putting up shelves, scraping the floors; the mother laboring over
  the white paint,
even the daughter coming from school to mop the century of
  scales and splatter from the cellar—
are both simple and complex because Sam T can tell you the an-
  swer to anything in the world
in one word and Sam F prefaces all his I-told-you-so's with "You
  don't understand, it's complex."
"It's simple," Sam T says, "where around here is anyone going to
  get money for toys?" The end.
Never mind the neighborhood's changing so fast that the new
  houses at the end of the block
are selling for twice what the whole block would have five years
  ago, that's not the point.
Business shits, right? Besides, the family—what's that they're eat-
  ing?—are wrong, right?
Not totally wrong, what are they, Arabs or something? but still,
  wrong enough, that's sure.
"And where do they live?" Sam F asks. "Sure as shit their last
  dime's in the lease and shit sure
they'll end up living in back of the store like gypsies, guaranteed:
  didn't I tell you or not

when the Minskys were still here that they'd bug out first chance
　　they got, and did they or no?"
Everyone thought the Minsky brothers would finally get driven
　　out of their auto repair shop
by zoning or by having their tools stolen so many times, Once,
　　Frank Minsky would growl,
on Yom Kippur, for crying out loud, but no, at the end, they just
　　sold, they'd worked fifty years,
And Shit, Frank said, that's fucking enough, we're going to
　　Miami, what do you want from me?
But Sam F still holds it against them, to cave in like that, the bug-
　　gers, bastards, shits . . .
What he really means, Sam, Sam, is that everyone misses the
　　Minskys' back room, where they'd head,
come dusk, the old boys, and there'd be the bottle of schnapps
　　and the tits from *Playboy*
in the grimy half-dark with the good stink of three lifetimes of
　　grease and sweat and bitching,
and how good that would be, back then, oh, how far back was
　　then? Last year, is that all?
"They got no class: shit, a toy store," Sam T says. What does that
　　mean, Sam? What class?
No class, that's all, simple: six months there and boom, they'll have a fire,
　　guaranteed.
Poor Sam, whether the last fire, at the only butcher store for
　　blocks the A&P hadn't swallowed,
was arson for insurance as Sam proved the next day, or whether,
　　the way the firemen saw it,
it was just a bum keeping warm in the alley, Sam's decided to take
　　it out on the strangers,
glaring at them over there in their store of dreams, their damned
　　pain-in-the-ass toy store.
What's the matter with you, are you crazy? is what the father finally
　　storms in with one afternoon,
both Sams turning their backs, back to their shit burgers, but old
　　Bernie himself is working today,
and *Hey*, Bernie says, *Don't mind them, they're just old shits, sit down, I'll*
　　buy you a coffee.

Who the fuck do they think they are? Here have a donut, don't worry, they'll be
all right,
and of course they will be. "In a month you won't get them out of
your hair," says Bernie,
and he's right again, old Bernie, before you know it Sam T has
got me cornered in the street.
"What is it, for Christ's sake, Sam? Let me go." "No, wait up, it's a
computer for kids."
"Sam, please, I'm in a hurry." "No, hold on, just a second, look, it's
simple."

About Brooklyn
1984

Brooklyn-Summer-Sunday
(fragment of part 4, translated from the Dutch by the author)

A walk after a late breakfast

Feeding on unaffordable food
or sleeping with a movie star
is probably, I said to her,
like living in a touristy neighborhood,

but still we walk to Sheepshead Bay.
The stream from Manhattan downtown
of living humans born brown
or becoming brown
carries us away,
strangers in a familiar
crowd

of American mouths that speak
Spanish, Russian and Greek
while from their youthful necks are swaying
unbearably black coffins full
of unbearably loud singing

to fill and overfill the heat
with waves of over-amplified
dialogues of band and beat

bouncing off the open bay
fade as they pass
followed by a new subway
train-full of human mass.

Brooklyn College Brain
1984

for David Shapiro & John Ashbery

You used to wear dungarees & blue workshirt,
sneakers or cloth-top shoes, & ride alone
on subways, young & elegant unofficial
bastard of nature, sneaking sweetness into Brooklyn.
Now tweed jacket & yr father's tie on yr breast,
salmon-pink cotton shirt & Swedish bookbag
you're half-bald, palsied lip & lower eyelid
continually tearing, gone back to college.
Goodbye Professor Ginsberg, get your identity
card next week from the front office so you can
get to class without being humiliated dumped on the
sidewalk by the black guard at the Student Union door.

Hello Professor Ginsberg have some coffee,
have some students, have some office hours
Tuesdays & Thursdays, have a couple subway tokens
in advance, have a box in the English Department,
have a look at Miss Sylvia Blitzer behind the typewriter
Have some poems er maybe they're not so bad have a
good time workshopping Bodhicitta in the Bird Room.

March 27, 1979

Fire in Luna Park
1985

The screaming produced by the great fright machines—
one like a dough beater that lifts, turns, plunges the victims
    strapped to its arms,
one a huge fluted pan that tries to whirl its passengers off the earth,
one that holds its riders upside down and pummels them until the
    screams pour out freely,
while above them the roller coaster, before it plunges, creeps
    seemingly lost among its struts and braces
and under them the Ghost Train jerks through tunnels here and
    there lighted by fluorescent bones—
has fallen still today.

To us who live on Lavender Bay,
formerly Hulk Bay, before that no one knows what,
it seemed the same easily frightened, big-lunged screamer vibra-
    toed in mock terror each night across the water, and we
    hardly heard and took no notice.
But last night the screams pierced through dinner parties' laugh-
    ter, lovemaking's crying, Mozart's laughing-and-crying, and
    kept at it, until we sat up startled.

The Ghost Train, now carrying seven souls and the baffled grief
    of families,
has no special destination,
but must wander looking for forgetfulness through the natural
    world,
where all are born, all suffer, and many scream,
and no one is healed but gathered and used again.

AMY CLAMPITT

Burial in Cypress Hills
1985

For Beverly and Lloyd Barzey

Back through East Flatbush, a raw grave
littered by the trashing of the social contract,
to this motel of the dead, its plywood and acrylic
itching gimcrack Hebrew like a brand name.

Her case botched by a vandal of a Brooklyn doctor,
she'd readied everything, had all the old snapshots
sorted, down to the last mysterious interior
obliterated in the processes of coming clear.

Surprising, the amount of privacy that opens,
for all the lifetime rub of other people,
around a name uncertified by being in the papers—
one mainly of the bilked, who never formed a party—

and how unhandsome the nub of actual survival.
Nobody is ever ready for the feel of the raw edge
between being and nothing, the knowledge
that abrades the palm, refusing to lie easy.

Yet something in the way the sun shines even now,
out in the open, on that final nugget, makes
bereavement blithe. The undertaker's deputy,
getting the latest lot of mourners into cars,

barks like a sergeant, as though even limbo must
be some new sort of boot camp. "Brooklyn people"—
one of the cousins sums it up, without rancor:
a way of doing business, part of the local color.

Burial in Cypress Hills, a place whose avenues
are narrower than anywhere in Brooklyn: dark-

boled gateposts crowded elbow to elbow,
the woodlot of innumerable burial societies,

each pair of verticals dense as a tenement
with names, or as a column in the *Daily Forward.*
Whoever enters here to take up residence
arrives an immigrant, out of another country.

The cortege, one of many, inches forward, no more
to be hurried than at Ellis Island. On foot now,
we find the yellow cellar hole, a window into clay,
without a sill, whose only view is downward.

Time, for the gravediggers, is unarguably money:
the cadence of their lifted shovelfuls
across the falling phrases of the Kaddish
strikes on a rarely opened vein of metal

whose pure ore rings like joy, although that's not
the name we've been conditioned into giving it.
Around us, flowering trees hang their free fabric,
incorporeal as the act of absolution. At our feet

an unintended dandelion breaks the hasp
of the adjoining plot's neglected ivy
to spend ungrudgingly its single
fringed medallion, alms for the sun.

From The Brooklyn Bridge
1985

2
(In memory of John Augustus Roebling, the designer of Brooklyn Bridge)

"The catenary curve is a natural
unity: perfect equilibrium,
perfect stability.

  *"It must not be
disturbed even for reasons of safety,
strength or economy.*

    "But what could disturb
a structure maintained by opposite
harmonising forces?

     "Not wind alone,
not water, not fire, not the earth alone.
All forces at rest in nature are at rest
because they spring from one source.

      "Their dynamic
universe is held in balance by a
constant play of energies and movements
originating from a disturbance
of rest, from single molecules one to
another.

  "Microcosmic unity
is a reflection of macrocosmic
harmony; totalities comprehended
by man's desire for the infinite.

       "It is
mathematically, spiritually,

mysteriously perceived and manifested
through an ideal: a system of diagonal
lines forming a hypoteneuse of a
right angle.

  "Like the catenary curve,
the triangle (which is geometrically
immovable) is a principle of
nature.

  "So much so that when catenary
curve (which is simultaneously an
inverted arch) and triangle are firmly
rooted to the earth, there is a quotient
of the highest order, representing
nature's laws and man's history.

    "There is
a perfect bi-system giving chaotic
passage a form linking it to its
destinies.

  "This perception of man's beauty
aspires toward divinity, through
lancet windows arched monumentally,
gateways, icons: uniting, identifying
in walls, fortresses, cathedrals.

      "One
such structure shifts the unique centre of
civilisation, salutes history,
provides a threshold to the future. It

"is a Hanging Garden, a Pyramid,
an Acropolis, an Athenaeum,
        "a Bridge . . ."

JOHN WAKEMAN

Love in Brooklyn
1985

"I love you, Horowitz," he said, and blew his nose.
She splashed her drink. "The hell you say," she said.
Then, thinking hard, she lit a cigarette:
"Not *love*. You don't *love* me. You like my legs,
and how I make your letters nice and all.
You drunk your drink too fast. You don't love *me*."

"You wanna bet?" he asked. "You wanna bet?
I loved you from the day they moved you up
from Payroll, last July. I watched you, right?
You sat there on that typing chair you have
and swung round like a kid. It made me shake.
Like once, In World War II, I saw a tank
slide through some trees at dawn like it was god.
That's how you make me feel. I don't know why."

She turned towards him, then sat back and grinned,
and on the bar stool swung full circle round.
"You think I'm like a tank, you mean?" she asked.
"Some fellers tell me nicer things than that."
But then she saw his face and touched his arm
and softly said "I'm only kidding you."

He ordered drinks, the same again, and paid.
A fat man, wordless, staring at the floor.
She took his hand in hers and pressed it hard.
And his plump fingers trembled in her lap.

MICHAEL S. HARPER

The Drowning of the Facts of Life
1985

Who knows why we talk of death
this evening, warm beyond the measure
of breath; it will be cool tomorrow
for in the waters off Long Beach
my brother's ashes still collect
the flowers of my mother and father,
my sister dropped in the vase
of a face they made of old places,
the text of water.

Tonight we talk of losses in the word
and go on drowning in acts of faith
knowing so little of humility,
less of the body,
which will die in the mouth of reality.

This foolish talk in a country
that cannot pronounce napalm
or find a path to a pool of irises
or the head of a rose.

My brother was such a flower;
he would spring into my path
on a subway train, above the ground
now, on the way home from school,
letting the swift doors pinch
his fingers of books and records,
house supplies from the corner market,
as he leaped back to the station
platform, crying his pleasure
to his brother,
who was on the train . . .
getting off at next exit
to look for him.

This is how we make our way home:
Each day when the Amtrak express
on the northeast corridor
takes my heritage from Boston
to the everglades of Maryland,
I think of the boy who sat
on the platform in the Canarsie,
on the uneven projects of New Lots
Avenue, BMT:

he was so small he could slip
through the swinging chains
of the express train
on the Williamsburg Bridge,
and not get touched by the third rail,
the chain link fencing of the accordion
swiveling to the swing and curses
of the motorman.

A fortnight my brother lay in coma,
his broken pate and helmet
in a shopping bag of effects,
his torn-off clothes and spattering
coins, the keys to the golden Yamaha—
with remnants of pavement in his scalp,
the trace of jacket laid under his head,
the black Continental idling
at anchor with the infinite,
the same black ice of the subway.

I came to chant over his fungus-
eaten flesh, allergic to his own
sweat, sweeter than the women
and children collecting
in caravan behind him; the Asian
nurses, so trained in the cadence
of thermometer and brain scan,
came in their green bracelets
and uniforms to relieve him—

a catheter of extract
makes the pomade of his hair
disappear, for his lips twitch
in remembrance at impact,
rage at the power of love,
the welcome table and the tabernacle
for his broken shoes and helmet.

Ponder the spent name of Jonathan,
apple and brother in the next
world, where the sacred text
of survival is buried in the bosom
of a child, radiated
in moonlight forever.
I touch the clean nostril
of the body in his mechanical
breathing, no chant sound enough
to light him from the rest
of contraption
to the syncopated dance of his name.

Tempest in Borough Park

1985

Come my
love, it is
the same whirlwind
which took Elijah
to heaven. Some lightnings
convert into chariots,
some into fire-horses. Let us
meet God like Elijah, stormwashed, cleanse
the light where smiling horrormongers stood.
The tempest is weary, fearing sleep, it still
keeps alive by dancing horas on the tired streets,
with feet of dust, hands of wind, the sphinx of Borough Park.
Last drops of rain, through sunset, are rainbow chasers. Itchy
cats, with fleas in their ears, piss gold: the terror of the ages.

DIANE KENDIG

Flatbush 1980: A State of the Caribbean in Brooklyn
1987

Five weeks there, I was a stranger among
strangers who accepted no one place home,
so carried it in shopping bags of yutiya and malanga,
Comidas chinas y latinas, on radios of salsa
and the Spanish floating everywhere
with no noun meaning "homesick," only
an awkward verb phrase "feel the less." All night
I heard it in the alleys and wakened in Madrid
or Coyoacan. By day I should have known better
but sought El Grecos, murals, huipils—
none of them any more indigenous to Brooklyn than I.
It was the language kept taking me,
kept filling me with elsewhere, kept filling
the every airwave of the island.

haiti. new york.

1988

this one morning
the dictator was gone
and brooklyn was singing
this one morning
caught in a flurry
of snow and imagination
down eastern parkway
towards the monument
of an unfinished
civil war.
this one morning
when the dictator
had fled death
with his crossboned
mask
moved over and
the haiti of brooklyn
spilled sweet champagne
into the contradictions
of the tiger's new year
the foam
drowning capsized boats
imprisonment
in their own country
imprisonment here
this one morning
when the dictator was gone
brooklyn wore its creole
manifestos
and the nurses and
the taxi drivers
and all the day maids all
had their day
of blue flags and red

waving
as tho
this one morning
the past could be shooed
with a wave in a
brooklyn snowstorm
and the footprints marching
towards the civil war monument
and the past sent marching
the past sent marching
towards the grave.

The Brooklyn Botanic Garden
1988

There was a rabbit face at dusk
And a double row of benches

Collecting in a shadow
Through which our footsteps tunneled.

The full moon
Dropped through a cloud,

Making me remember how you blinked
When a drop of rain

Hit your cheek, and I kissed it
Before it could fall,

Later wondering if it would have fallen
Or just disappeared.

Then we were trying to kiss
With our eyes open,

The dark pools
Deepening into each other

Until we could see
The second of loss closing in.

Running through this fast snow
Past the frozen pond,

What comes back is
How we spoke of spring returning

The water lilies
As we watched them slowly

Dying last autumn,
When I began to want you in my life

And confuse you
With the yellow lily.

ALAN DUGAN

Boast
1989

I've walked every walkable bridge
into and out of Manhattan and climbed
the towers of Brooklyn Bridge twice
and gotten the grease of the Roeblings' cables
all over my hands, face, and raincoat,
drunk illegally up there where the cables
groan on their supporting high rollers
    Hurray
and now I'm crippled in Manhattan, played out.

Should I have done a Brody
when I had the high body
rather than lie here in a flat?
No. Rather I celebrate the rain-
storm over the East River that night
that kept the police indoors
and lit the bridge with burning water
back to Brooklyn where I was born.

Introduction to the Telephone
1989

The telephone rang in the grocery store
and the grocery man said Answer it.
I was six years old and did. I said
Hello to the black mouth on the wall
and the black ear screamed in my ear.
I dropped it scared as he laughed
and I lost my telephone virginity
to the black howling universe of wire
looping out the plate-glass window, down
the Brooklyn avenue to New York City:
there, a vampire self of words sucks
money from that wire world, but I
am sick because it bit me in the ear.
I am adult to the instrument
and listen to the women angels' voices
calling the cities by their given names.

STANLEY BARKAN

On the Milkboxes
1989

(*For Howard Strassman*)

On the milkboxes
in front of the old
grocery store

where junkmen
jangled:
"we cash clothes"

and ices men
came with all
their foreign fruits
rainbowing
our appetites

and knish kings
rolled crisp
and hard-edged
squares of dough

and you and I
and all the huckleberry
gang played nuts
against chalk-scrawled walls

and Shimbo
incised deep shimmies
in the spring-warm asphalt

playing banker-broker
after the tossing
of bundles
of baseball tickets

and slide of soda caps
in the skelly square

and all the strings
of milk-wires
spread from room-to-room
house-to-house
along the rooftops
of our minds

and pigeons cooed
in their chicken-mesh coops
and stickball tosses
over the third level
of the Great Gas Storage Tank

and elevated trains
jostled their way
to old bathhouses

in the tinsel
cotton-candied days
of Coney & Playland

and the first bikes
rolled
their hooping wheels
all the way to Canarsie

and the passing
of chow mein & chop suey trays
through inner-courtyard windows.

There we spoke of everything:
"Ask me anything!" you defied . . .

On the milkboxes
in front of the old grocery store.

MICHAEL WATERS

Brooklyn Waterfall
1989

Water where you least expect it:
   swelling every closet,
      tumbling down stairwells,

raining through light
   fixtures onto night tables . . .
      my good Aunt Beatrice,

ever forgetful, had twisted
   the faucet handle fully,
      plugging the drain

with a red rubber stopper,
   then set off to shop.
      If water can be joyous,

imagine the unfettered
   revelry: no one home,
      the glorious, porcelain

plashing from the third
   story so loud, abandoned,
      anticipatory.

By the time she piddled
   Saturday morning away,
      the water had traveled

miles—no slow, molten
   flow, but unabashed
      raveling, elemental motion.

So when my aunt looked up
from her swollen mop,
my father stormed back out,

the water trailing him
to the local tavern.
He swilled it with bourbon.

How far he managed to float away
from his fearful, weeping family,
or for how many hours,

I don't remember, but
he swayed home later,
muttered *what the hell,*

and joined the communal
sweeping, work that keeps
a family together, water

still seeping into the earth
where it waits for us,
not needing forgiveness.

PART VIII

1990s

Daniel Hall
Enid Dame
Kimiko Hahn
Hugh Seidman
Steven Hartman
David Gershator
Donna Masini
Patricia Spears Jones
Hayden Carruth
Fran Castan
Quentin Rowan
Vijay Seshadri
Juanita Brunk
Cornelius Eady
Rika Lesser
Goran Tomcic
Hettie Jones
Philip Levine
Sapphire
Shulamit

Prospect Park
1990

Each week another ad begins:
"Inbound D train, Monday morning,
you sat across from me, reading
the *Voice* (or were you?) . . ." and ends
in a rubble of numbers. That "you"
might be capitalized, refined
out of the temporal. Between the lines
a secret blinks: I already know You

will not write, You will not call . . .
Midnight, a racket filters up:
work never done, the writer mad
to finish, to savor the full stop
following the parenthetical
question, thus: ?).

ENID DAME

Riding the D-Train
1991

Notice the rooftops,
the wormeaten Brooklyn buildings.
Houses crawl by,
each with its private legend.
In one, a mother
is punishing her child
slowly, with great enjoyment.
In one, a daughter
is writing a novel
she can't show to anyone.

Notice your fellow riders:
the Asian girl chewing a toothpick,
the boy drawing trees on his hand,
the man in a business suit
whose shoes don't match.

Everything is important:
that thin girl, for instance,
in flowered dress, golden high heels.
How did her eyes get scarred?
Why is that old man crying?
Why does that woman carry
a cat in her pocketbook?

Don't underestimate
any of it.

Anything you don't see
will come back to haunt you.

ENID DAME

Soup
1991

For Josh Waletzsky

1.

I am making chicken soup in the Vilna Ghetto.
You think it's easy? First
you've got to sneak in the chickens
feather by feather bone by bone and then the vegetables
root by root leaf by leaf next, the salt
past the Jewish police at the gate, and the Lithuanians,
the Nazis over their shoulders. You've got to be careful.
I keep the soup pot alive in the Vilna Ghetto
while all around buildings simmer
with meetings: young people, Zionists, leftists, rightists,
Communists, Bundists. My brother
tells me I'm on the wrong track.

He is sneaking guns into the Vilna Ghetto
part by part scrap by scrap and then the explosives.
This isn't easy, he says, but it's necessary.
Think of the working class, think of the revolution.
Think of the heroes at Warsaw, think of the pits at Ponar.
All we need here is a little solidarity.
All we need now is one good uprising.

2.

She is sneaking Jews out of the Vilna Ghetto
into the forest man by man woman by woman
(there are no children left, no Jewish children).
The leader, a Jew with a Russian name, Yurgis,
doesn't like it at all.
But what can he do?
She is a hero, I guess. Here she is on TV,
on the documentary my daughter watches.

Me, I was somewhere nearby. I was making soup in the forest
for the Partisans, the peasants, the Jews, the Russians.
(I left my brother, he left me, back in the ghetto.)
Here, we trapped some rabbits, dug up a few wild scallions.
Yadwiga found us some mushrooms.
(They looked poisonous, but tasted like pine trees.)

3.

I am warming up soup in Brooklyn,
in Brighton Beach, down by the worn-out ocean.
It's tomato-egg-drop soup from the Chinese take-out,
around the corner, next to the Russian deli
(where the man hums rock 'n' roll, counts change in Yiddish).
Beside me, my daughter watches the TV program.
I watch the tears break out on her face like a rash.
Why is she crying? What can she know of that time?
Me, all my tears are locked up behind my eyes,
rusted like all the words
in the mother language I don't even dream in now.
Me, I don't cry.

Me, I survive and survive.
How I survive! I've outlasted Vilna and Ponar,
the meetings the sewer the forest
the Judenrat and my family
(except for this one, who came later).

My brother stares at us suddenly out of the screen,
out of that photograph I always hated.
He's 20, he's serious, his ears are too big.
I can't look. I turn my back. I lower the flame
under the saucepan, the soup shouldn't burn.
You think it's easy, to concentrate on details?
Details, let me tell you, keep you alive.
Details, I thank God for them.

My daughter looks ugly and old, her face all muddy.
They've got someone else on there now, another story.

I could tell stories too, but I never talked much.
He talked all the time. He scattered his words like salt.
Words, he said, words are important, words can change things.
He sneaked his words in past the guards, he whispered, he
    shouted.
Think of the Jewish people, he said and he disappeared.
(And the Nazi troop train blew up, and they blamed the
    Russians.)

She's crying harder, my daughter; sobs choke in her throat like
    fishbones.
"Mama," she says, "Mama, why didn't you tell me?"
I say, "What's to tell? Have some soup."

Crossing Neptune Ave.
1992

I recall spotting the couple
at Coney Island, the wife's face
bright and fragrant
as salt
but too when I reached home
the chocolate turtles I bought
had burst open
crawling with white insects.
I didn't get sick.
I promptly forgot about it
and thought of him surrounded
by flurries
on the beach.

Yes, Yes, Like Us

1992

In the BAM Opera House,
before the "impressive" audience,
Wilson's nineteenth-century, dream-tableau Gilgamesh.

At intermission, an older man
gave a tempting woman his number and name
(heroic if futile, I thought, enviously).

But still, the people were tall.
Had I shrunk?
Had I always been small before the unattainable?

For I confess, the bare-breasted, thick-braided
blond actress of the whore got me hot,
who seduced Enkidu the hunter.

Though I gave none my number or name,
but rode the express with the rest,
back under the river.

At Wall Street a pack of kids seemed murderous, if given a
      chance.
Yes, yes, like us,
if given a chance.

Yes, yes, back home last night
on the black leather couch in the halogen light,
I counted my enemies, counted my friends.

In sleep too,
I credited and debited
the ledgers of enmity and allegiance.

And woke to Gilgamesh still counting coup.
To what end? but that I had knelt
To scour the kitchen linoleum.

Because my father battled the universe's much-quoted
death by disorder,
which only heroic Gilgamesh shall conquer.

Mother's Day, Coney Island: Metropolitan Jewish Geriatric Home

1992

And veins web her temples,
and my father pins on the orchid,
and my card names her the best mother.

But Alzheimer's or arteriosclerosis (the end is the same)
praises him ad nauseam,
but accuses my absence, my silence.

And if he leaves she calls me Monas,
or if the nurse asks: Is this Hugh?
she only says: Hugh is Hugh.

Nor can she think where she sleeps,
but: Somewhere, if no one is there.
And she licks her lip and pulls her sock,

and, silent, I am her judgment
before the memorial brass plaques and the Atlantic,
relived later like a film.

And here lie the projects,
ruined by the blacks, my father says—
the provider, in anger, who now cannot provide.

Yet we must share a cab back with a black man,
who mourns to hear of her,
as we mourn his bankrupt grocery.

Though then my father argues the fare,
again as if anger mattered.
And he says that she loves me,

that their lives are over, that it is my turn to live.
And I hear his voice of despair
that may speak to no one.

But how shall the nova not implode?
Or the wave vault not fall?
As there the steel mushroom of the obsolete Parachute Jump

looms on the world,
whose fliers I envied with awe as a child,
set free till silk bore them down.

The Future of Patriotic Poems

1992

> *Blind hoboes sell American flags*
> *And bad poems of patriotism*
> *On Saturday evenings forever in the rain*
> JAMES WRIGHT

I travel on the B16
thru the bowels of Brooklyn.
The only black person on this bus
is the driver.
Everytime I return to Bay Ridge
I'm nearly tricked into believing
I'm back in Storm Lake
although we never had Sicilian ices
or Greek gyros.

The bus drops me off
near the Wiesner Gallery.
I hear men read poems
about persecution & forgiveness
with as many accents
as in the Casbah or U.N.
Today, a Russian immigrant
sings an ode to the Statue of Liberty
proving how wrong I was
to think patriotic poems are dead
or that everyone hates Brooklyn.

DAVID GERSHATOR

For Walt and the Lion Tamers
1995

First ran into you
hiding out around Bushwick Public Library
I was in love puppy love with a young blonde librarian
stamping long litanies of date dues
she loved my first after-shave lotion
touched me touched your book
made me blush and come back
for more date dues

Public library had small concrete lions out front
what a rush of lines and lions!
verse after verse you devoured me!
I was raw and you ate me raw
you got to my bones and sucked them clean
turned them into panpipes in a tenement
where the only pipes I knew
were cold radiators and faulty plumbing
man, you had me

Later someone tarred the lions
still later someone smashed the lions
later still they up and disappeared
it's tough to be a lion in Bushwick Brooklyn
library lions don't stand a chance
in the man eating streets
they went just like this
the neighborhood went just like that
gone with the lions to some landfill

Sometimes, Walt, I still see you around
working in a shelter for the homeless
I still keep in touch with your Leaves
first touched in a leafless slum
where grass was out of bounds

where I was ashamed to bring a friend or a date
but I wasn't ashamed to bring you keep you renew you
pay your date due fines bail you out
always tempted to steal you

I knew that you knew me inside out
I touched you touched a man
I would've loved to touch the librarian
but what's a blonde compared to a book, Walt
I knew you'd outlast the damn lions

Getting Out of Where We Came From
1994

I was born in Brooklyn.
Even the birds were dingy
and the dark courtyard between
buildings filled with grimy light
like the lit up inside of a pumpkin.
There we could be frantic.
There we could stamp and spin
or fall down pretending to be dead.
It is still the place my father loves.
I see him: slicing meats,
stampeding streets in wild teenage goodboy crowds,
so near to me, on the lip of my dream
green workclothes still oil the air
of my bedroom, saturate the walls.
He works hard for you seven days a week.
In 1963 grease-soaked, shadowed, we ferried the harbor
to a new duplex. The model home.
Barbecues, mortgages. *Where will we get the money?*
The bridge went up. The basement flooded.
Up to our knees in water we bailed and bailed.
In their yards the neighbors laughed
and drank and shook their heads, *Too bad
they didn't know the house was built on swamp.*

Giants in the Earth

1994

I walk at night, the city building and breaking around me,
over cracked concrete, over broken pavement, over steel plates
the ground bumpy, uneven beneath me.
I listen for the joy inside my bones,
the steady, even transportation of my blood.
I go down to watch the trucks, the men climb into the earth,
the pulse and rhythm of the city slower, the cadence looser.
Soon I am among them: builders, diggers, sweating their nightly
    excavations;
sandblast, jackhammer, the city making itself over, sloughing off
    layers.
I love the way things get built at night: people, the body rebuild-
    ing itself,
bone, tissue, and skin, the cells of the dermis, the pumping
    digestions,
the networks of neuron, dendrite, the bustle of the dream pulse.

Caterpillar. FIAT ALIA. Dynahoe 490.
Week by week the machinery moves across Delancey Street,
closer to the river where the pulse begins, slowly,
as I imagine dinosaurs moved. Heavy legs over mud and vegeta-
    tion.

The forklift moves forward, lifts, as a priest raises a chalice.
Dynahoe 490 swivels to face it.
A man leans in his seat, grips the wheel, grasps the shift,
lifts the claw to raise the long arm,
claws a clump of rocky concrete to the street below,
the teams of men still digging around him. He
lifts shifts dumps, lifts shifts dumps,
the torchlights of the welders sparking in the dug-out hole
against the black night, bridge lights, four bent men circle
a trashcan fire, warming themselves, whisking their hands back
    from the sparks.
And the sparks flying out of the ground look like hell splintering.

Now it seems they are breaking the city down:
streets, trees, buildings coming down; broken lives, lines to fami-
    lies broken;
breaking down buildings and grandfathers, bridges, traditions,
the uprooted on their corners.
Thirty-two-year-old men in their beds.

Dreams are the places roots rock.
It comes to me now, one of those nonplaces the mind keeps
returning to: the empty lot at the edge of Brooklyn, cracked glass
    and gravel,
bent cans, tampon wrappers, the overpass, the echo beneath,
and no one to hear it except the screaming child, the projects
    sulking in the distance.
As some knew tree, fish, bird, the patterns and habits,
I knew brick and concrete, glass and light,
the diamond sidewalks that burned in the summers,
round-stoned walkways that shone in the rain,
the cement walk, boxed squares for handball, slate blocks thrust
    up by the movement of trees.

The vibration of jackhammers thrills me, shatters me.
That something could be made of all this breaking.
Sweet rain and sweat and the lovely yellow machinery knocking,
the black gravel curved as the shell of a turtle.

I stand a long time watching them, lean across the fissure into a
    wood-slat hole.
A man's red eyes glow up at me. He grins, unhooks the lamp
    from his belt and climbs out of the ground.

Sometimes it feels like it's me breaking apart.

What is the name of that truck, that tool?
What are you making? Where are your children?
What is the sound of a body breaking, the cells rebuilding, the
    heart deteriorating?

The forklift turns.
A shovel falls against the truck's flank.
Below the streetlife, above the subway systems, the iron girders
     brace,
and still the machinery plunges, breaking ground, turning the
     dirt, tenderly, as you'd lift a lover's buttock;
steel pipes like metal pelvises scattered across the pavement,
the banging of tools falling in a strange blue light.

Halloween Weather (a Suite)
1995

First Frost

In the booth across from me at Tom's Diner,
three Irish detectives talk about food and service.
They loudly denounce Brooklyn's lack of cuisine
and exult the glories of seafood in Myrtle Beach.

One guy says over and over
as he digs deeper into his banana walnut pancakes,
I could take it or leave it, but now
I just gotta have dessert.
Used to be 50/50,
but now I just gotta have it.

In the next block, the crack children
drift so fast they become wild clouds,
storm clouds swifter than the wind,

while up near the corner of Washington
and Sterling, their elders drink and drink
as the "oldies" station plays Smokey in his
twenties.

All week it's been Halloween weather,
still summer warm, but there's that hiss
from the North
chill.

Prayer

There are words that refuse me;
hermeneutics, tensile, circadian.

They feel like old expensive furniture
lovingly made for little use.

No, I should have learned them at eighteen
the way I learned to drink cheap wine.

No money again, just the usual dire straits
sharp dry leaves turn cyclone mean
and the full moon already gone.

Halloween weather, words of no use—
A mirror on the war within or just a popular song.

A tall poor Black man fiercely holds his elaborate CD player
as it outblasts all the obscenities on Vanderbilt Avenue.

And I know every one of them
by heart.

Down on my knees or down on my luck.
Lord, oh lord, deliver me.

Day of the Dead

Here is Brooklyn
here are the Anglos
here is the Day of the Dead

This makes sense, what with
all the blood spilled in battles
from Sheepshead Bay to Red Hook.
Not even a microscopic mention in the *Times*
unless five or more bats are used
to beat down the young men, mostly
Black, White, Hispanic
English-speaking?

So all these well-traveled people have brought back
perfect rituals appropriate really to the desert
and hills of Mexico. But we have our deserts,
our hills. Our bluffs and valleys too. Our bridges, our tunnels
and those subterranean maps like Escher's etchings—
rational schematics for daily trekking

from island to island
dream to dream.

So dressed in black from head to toe
we walk as if from one funeral to another
from Christian hymns to Buddhist sutras
always in this weather, a casual regard
for the walk from one street to the other
breathing the sugar-cube skeletons
happy for the privilege.

The Hyacinth Garden in Brooklyn
1996

A year ago friends
    took me walking
on the esplanade
    in Brooklyn. I've
no idea where it
    was, I could never
find it on my own.
    And as we walked,
looking out over
    the water, a sweet
aroma came to us,
    heavy and rich,
of a hyacinth
    garden set
on the landward side
    among apartment
houses, a quite large
    garden with flowers
of every size and color,
    and the famous
perfume filled the air.
    It surrounded me,
dazed me, as I stood
    by the rail looking
down. There vaguely
    among the blooms
I saw Hyacinthus,
    the lovely African
boy beloved by Apollo,
    lying there, dying,
the dark body already
    rotting, melting
among flowers, bleeding
    in Brooklyn, in

Paradise, struck down
  by the quoit thrown
by the grief-stricken god,
  an African boy
chosen for beauty, for love,
  for death, fragrance
beside the water
  on the esplanade
somewhere in Brooklyn,
  in Paradise.

FRAN CASTAN

Authority

1996

My grandmother was beaten
by her own father for reading
in the wrong language. In Zhitomir,
in the *shtetl,* you could read
Hebrew or Yiddish, not Russian.
If you were a girl,
you need only read enough
to light the Shabbos candles
or say the holiday prayers.
Grandmother yearned for beauty,
squeezed elderberries into whitewash,
painted her room until it glowed
pink as clouds above the setting sun.
Who did she think she was,
trading her father's rice
for a Russian book?

My mother was always reading.
Daughter of her mother,
what choice did she have?
Each week she walked
to the New Utrecht Branch
of the Brooklyn Public Library.
Mother yearned for knowledge.
She read the latest theories
of child care. The authors were men,
a new breed. Experts
who invented "The Feeding Schedule,"
a four-hour interval
they pronounced "Ideal."

As my cries grew to howls,
as her tender breasts
engorged, Mother watched the clock,

dutifully waiting, earnestly wanting us
to be models of the new order.
When the merciful fourth hour concluded
and I had cried myself
through stages of distress
to a fitful sleep, she would wake me.
It would take a long time
to trust the body I found myself in
to bring forth my own voice
as if, for the first time, it could be heard.
Granddaughter and daughter
of these women, I am usually writing.
What choice do I have?

Prometheus at Coney Island
1996

Up over the swell of hot sugar
up over the swell of rubber
Up over the death creaks, rises and falls
like heart attacks
Up over the backyards and bricks
Up over the smell of Ms. Roha's beans
Up over fat men in boxer shorts
Up over the people in ticket stands
Who hate you.
Up over the haunted houses and
1942 ectoplasm.
Up over the Coney Island gray beach,
over the Coney Island gray water that will
make your shins itch.
Up and turning,
circling back over the city, back over pipes
and billboards, pressures and nausea;
our car turns and sways and equilibriums
like greased jets and leather.
Over the swell of hot sugar at Coney Island
they pulled him hard,
under a yellow snow-line:
Gesticulating without talking,
creaking like the shingles of an ancient house,
raising and lowering like breath
sighing farewell to its ancient patriarch
blowing kisses as he's taken away,
like a famed entertainer heaving in the public eye.
            In the impaling sun
they threw him into the sea of
Pomatum grease,
        to singe his beard and
rid him of his dirt.
            Watermelons and pumpkins

were brought, and a pipe of brass to keep cool
his face—so as to show sick
newborn smartness,
        an avatar
of polka dancers.
          And laid out was an accordion
and Pannish mouth harp
under which clasped women could dance in the
sand—
moaning over containers overrun with fruit and fish.
Under the figure eights of gulls—
decorating the sand's own dead hills,
lighting fire in the company of thrills,
as was life in the old country.

VIJAY SESHADRI

Street Scene
1996

The job of redemption, with its angels and lawyers,
runs late into the morning;
the halls are empty, and from sea green foyers
where aquamarine jackets sag unused
no one walks out to be disabused
by the day, so confident and businesslike.
The domiciled, stunned, paralyzed, in mourning

for the vanishing illuminations, radium-edged,
that made their nerve ends glow
in the dark, are secretly pledged
to attenuate themselves in this,
the spirit's nocturnal crisis,
and still twitch with dreamwork,
and won't open their eyes. But although

not enough energy otherwise subsists
for the nurse to pop an antihistamine
and rise from her viral mists,
for the existential tough guy and thief
to wake up to some extra grief,
for the dog to be led to the park,
for the *viejo* to paint his fire escape green,

so that their race might never be caused to perish
from the contradictions of flight,
up above the satellite dish
pigeons of every color but exactly one size
mob, scatter, and reorganize
to practice crash landings on the street
that divides the black neighborhood from the white.

And at a distance rinsed of charity and malice,
their riots are being umpired by

the unmentionable, porticoed phallus
of the Williamsburg Savings Bank clock tower,
which manufactures the next hour,
serene in an ongoing function
it can never be called on to abjure or justify.

On this Earth
1996

To love my own, my body,
to know without saying, *legs, you are good legs,*
and feet and stomach and arms, good, and the spaces
under my arms, and the brown pigments
splashed across my back like tea leaves.
To love my body the way
I sometimes love a stranger's: a woman
on the subway, tired, holding her two bags,
a child slumped against her like another sack
as the train stops and starts and the child says something
so quietly no one else can hear it,
but she leans down, and whispers back,
and the child curls closer. I would love my body
the way a mother can love her child, or the way
a child will love anyone
who gives it a home on this earth, a place
without which it would be nothing, a dry branch
at the window of a lit room.

Dread

1997

I'm going to tell you something
It's a simple fact of life.
If you're a young man in East New York,
Here's a simple fact of life:
If they don't shoot you with a gun,
They'll cut you with a knife.

I'm standing at the grave
Of a just-buried friend,
Staring at the fresh mound
Of a just-buried friend.
Don't know how it got started,
Can't see where it'll end.

Looked for a glass of water
But they gave me turpentine
You can ask for a glass of water
All you'll get is turpentine
I don't know why this life
Is like askin' a brick for wine.

I've lost eight friends already,
Who'll make number nine?
Lord, buried eight friends already,
Who'll be number nine?

I'd love to make plans with you, Sugar,
But I don't believe we'll have the time.

I sleep with the bullet
That didn't have my name,
Say *good morning* to the bullet
That didn't have my name,
So when my number comes up, baby,
It'll be the one thing you can't blame.

536 Saratoga Avenue

1997

Driving by it now—walking in Brownsville
is no longer safe—536 remains
the only semi-private house on the block.
Everything else has changed: The tenements
across the street are gone. Nothing
replaces them. On our side, burnt and
blown-out frames surround empty courtyards.

Long before I was born, my mother's family
bought the house. Grandmother Ruchtcha died.
I bear the English name she took at
Immigration. Had she not died, I would be
someone else—a name is powerful.

Sharing a bedroom with my middle sister,
I wondered why the playroom was not my own.
Too young to remember Grandfather's moving
out. He lived nearby, across a busy street,
then in the downstairs flat, then in a "home."
Finally, he lived with us; the playroom his again.

My eldest sister had the long front room.
In the street you knew when she talked
on the telephone: she'd stick her feet
out the jalousie windows. Now a wide
strip of tape masks a bifurcation.

Of course, there were other rooms, other doors,
but one of those farthest back completes the tour.

The full bath was called "Rika's bathroom"
because I hogged it. In my sleep I'd walk there.
Awake I'd drown my toys, imagining the room
to be an island. Shipwrecked, I allowed myself

a large box of cream-filled cookies. With water,
soft towels, the clothing in the hamper,
I'd do all right. I won't allow myself to imagine
what goes on there now. What the small black boy,
who rode a tricycle when we drove past
last summer, would think if he found
scratched with the head of safety-pin
on the tile wall beneath the towel rod
my name.

GORAN TOMCIC

The Fire

1997

I think I was trying
to figure out which way is South.
I think I was imagining nightswimming,
miniature plankton illuminated by the moon.
I think I was watching the planes
flying low over Williamsburg.
I think I was scraping the old layers of paint.
I think I was scraping the layers of you
in me. Not me—my heart wept
like a volcano, in flames.

You Are What You Eat
1998

For Margaret Wolf

If a plant could be
a tough bird
the prize would go
to Dirty Crazy Mean Mike's
honeysuckle,
which grew
on the blood and bones of all
our dead animals, buried
against a fence on Fifth Street

Thrived despite Mike's filthy garage
and survived to spread in Brooklyn.

    All that time
it was the smell and how
I used to suck
        the sweet

        nights I thought
        I'd die too
        of love or loneliness

and now this Brooklyn boy
pulls down a pistil
its one crystal droplet intact
"the thing made real" gleaming under the sun

and I think of Dirty Mike's
greasy planting hands gone

gone the guinea pig, gone
the rabbit, the dogs who
shat there, even the bird
dead at the hands of the cats

manna in my mouth

The Unknowable
1999

Practicing his horn on the Williamsburg Bridge
hour after hour, "woodshedding" the musicians
called it, but his woodshed was the world.

The enormous tone he borrowed from Hawkins
that could fill a club to overflowing
blown into tatters by the sea winds

teaching him humility, which he carries
with him at all times, not as an amulet
against the powers of animals and men

that mean harm or the lure of the marketplace.
No, a quality of the gaze downward
on the streets of Brooklyn or Manhattan.

Hold his hand and you'll see it, hold his eyes
in yours and you'll hear the wind singing
through the cables of the bridge that was home,

singing through his breath—no rarer than yours,
though his became the music of the world
thirty years ago. Today I ask myself

how he knew the time had come to inhabit
the voice of the air and how later
he decided the time had come for silence,

for the world to speak any way it could?
He wouldn't answer because he'd find
the question pompous. He plays for money.

The years pass, and like the rest of us
he ages, his hair and beard whiten, the great
shoulders narrow. He is merely a man—

after all—a man who stared for years
into the breathy unknowable voice
of silence and captured the music.

Some Different Kinda Books
1999

I

She asks why we always
read books about black people.
(I spare her the news she is black.)
She wants something different.
Her own book is written in pencil.
She painstakingly goes back & corrects
the misspelled words.
We write each day.
Each day the words look like
a retarded hand from Mars
wrote them.
Each day she asks me how
do you spell: didn't, tomorrow, done
husband, son, learning, went, gone . . .
I can't think of all the words she can't spell.
It's easier to think of what she can spell:
MY NAME IS CARMEN LOPEZ.
I am sorry I was out teacher.
My husband was sick.
You know I never miss school.
In that other program
I wasn't learning nothing.
Here, I'm learning so I come.
What's wrong with my husband?
I don't know. He's in the hospital. He's real sick
I was almost out the room
when I hear the nurse ask him,
Do you do drugs?
He say yes.
I say what!
I don't know nuthin' 'bout no drugs.
I'm going off in the hospital.

He's sick.
I'm mad.

Nobody tells you nuthin'!
I didn't hear that nurse
I wouldn't know
nuthin'.
Huh?
Condoms? No, teacher.
He's my husband.
I never been with another man.

II

I think he got AIDS
he still don't tell me.
I did teacher. I tried
to read the chart at the hospital
but I couldn't figure out those words.
Doctor don't say, he say privacy.
The nurse tell me.
She's Puerto Rican. She say your husband
got AIDS.
I go off in the hospital.
Nobody tell me nuthin'.
He come home.
He say it's not true,
he's fine.
He's so skinny without his clothes
he try to hide hisself nekkid
don't want me to look.
I say you got to use
one of those things.
He say nuthin's wrong.
with him.

III

He stop sayin' that.
Now he just say he's gonna die

all the time
all the time
dying.
I say STOP that talk,
the doctor say you could
live a long time
my sister-in-law say,
he got it so you got it
it's like that.
I say, I don't got it,
my kids don't got it either.
Teacher, I need a letter for welfare
that I'm coming to school
on a regular basis.

IV

He's in P.R.,
before that he started messing around
again.
Over the Christmas holidays
he died.
That's where I was at
in P.R.
I'm fine. Yeah, I'm sure teacher.
What do *I* wanna do teacher?
I just wanna read some different
kinda books.

Brooklyn Bodhisattvas
1999

Brooklyn babes,
nubile, then pregnant,
dream of fine china,
a spandex-sleek ass,
and the high regard
of the highly regarded.

When the children,
grow to be the shadows
of the dream,
and what is lost is lost,
anxiety diminishes.

No time like the present.

Without gurus, mandalas
and celibacy
the Buddha belly laugh
arises out of unalloyed joy,
love suffuses and infuses,
and with easy grace,
cozy conversations
begin with the Angel of Death.

PART IX

Twenty-first Century

Joanna Fuhrman	Marjorie Maddox
Martín Espada	Maggie Nelson
Timothy Liu	Martín Espada
Jonathan Galassi	Tom Sleigh
Jessica Greenbaum	Anne Pierson Wiese
Robert Hershon	Vijay Sheshadri
Donald Lev	Karen Alkalay-Gut
Jerry Wemple	John Skoyles
Ed Barrett	Daniel Tobin
Lisa Jarnot	Matthew Lippman
Joshua Beckman	Michael Morse
Noelle Kocot	Nuar Alsadir
D. Nurkse	Andrea Baker
Ed Ochester	Mary DiLucia
Jeffrey Harrison	Jonah Winter
Matthew Rohrer	David Margolis
Agha Shahid Ali	Joelle Hann
D. Nurkse	Anthony Lacavaro
L. S. Asekoff	Alicia Jo Rabins
Katherine Lederer	Georgine Sanders
Marilyn Hacker	Melissa Beattie-Moss

JOANNA FUHRMAN

Freud in Brooklyn

2000

Sigmund Freud is walking out
of the picture. His feet cut off. His face
blurred by the shadow of his fedora's rim.
He looks away toward the Atlantic.
The ocean is just a gray smudge,
the size of an index finger's tip.

Freud traveled to New York mainly
to see Coney Island's Dreamland Park.
He had read about the fake tenements there,
burned down twice a day for Lower East Side immigrants
to gawk, and about the newborns in the incubator exhibit,
pink and wrinkled as a vulture's cheek,
their names written on the glass in bubble print.
Freud became obsessed with the Coney Island lion,
"so huge the concrete under him had cracked,"
read the *Tagezeitung*, and with
the thousand glass cranes in the glass house
and with the fantasy ride on Pike's Pier,
the three dimensional panorama of Hell.

In Hell, Freud read, the tourist enters a boat
and descends. He's soon surrounded
by pink glass flames, a Bach toccata
and a tunnel painted with a mural of judgment day,
Jesus standing on a *trompe l'oeil* cloud,
his gold robes weightless in the wind.
Candles light up his eyes.
When the tourist feels he's about to leave,
a trumpet sounds and thirty papier mâché devils fall.

In Vienna, Freud dreams about Coney Island's Hell.
His eyes close and he enters the boat,
feels it seal around him like a skin.

Each devil has the face of a different patient.
First, the wolf man baring his teeth.
Then Anna O. grinning.
Freud says "Come with me in my sleek new boat."
They say very sweetly "no."

At this, he wakes and puts on his slippers
trudges to his terrace.
It's May, the pale azaleas are half
on the branch, half torn
under the wooden wheels of old buggies.
He watches children playing in the street.
A girl with a sash over her eyes spins
until she falls down laughing.

When Freud's ship docks in New York,
Dreamland has already started burning.
Something about the hot tar was off
and set the park on fire.

Heaven's soon ablaze.
The angels' wings melt. God on his throne
with his fake gold scepter explodes in a giant roar,
starting the burning in Hell.
The glass flames turn the fire blue.
The devils vanish as they touch the flame.
Even the wet boats burn,
the water under them black as char.

As Freud checks into his room
on East Fourteenth Street,
much of the park is ash.
The burning inches toward the famous lion
as he paces in his wrought iron Art Nouveau cage.
The tamer stands frozen, watching for awhile,
and then, out of love, he shoots.

The Mexican Cabdriver's Poem
For His Wife, Who Has Left Him

2000

We were sitting in traffic
on the Brooklyn Bridge,
so I asked the poets
in the backseat of my cab
to write a poem for you.

They asked
if you are like the moon
or the trees.

I said no,
she is like the bridge
when there is so much traffic
I have time
to watch the boats
on the river.

The Brooklyn Botanic Garden
2000

Edenic glory sequestered inside fifty-two
acres flanking three-and-a-half billion years
of life transplanted along that crowded
Trail of Evolution—fat-free Häagen-Dazs
licked down to the stick by summer waddlers
taking a stroll across a Japanese bridge
backdropped by an endless Latinate fleet
sprouting up like spores throughout the park
with nomenclature diverting our eyes from
sepals fuzzed with dew—a bumble bee
oblivious to this need to classify what is
not ours to own—that slab of concrete
balm enough for any city-dwelling financier
praying the Dow won't fall while roses
spill their petals over these dusty paths
pelted by sudden grape-sized drops of rain—
our senses reawakening now to a steady
sibilant stream of Sunday car exhaust
along the perimeter—unseen subway trains
tunneling under gothic eyesores fenced-
out by that Fragrance Garden for the blind.

View

2000

Isabel, I have been pushing you
for more than half an hour on this playground
horse as high as it safely goes—
which isn't nearly high enough for you.
The rain is just holding off, or not quite just,
which means we're by ourselves in this place
that's usually thronged on a late-spring
Brooklyn Sunday afternoon
with fathers doing their weekend fathering
(some trying to doze, or sneak a look at the paper
between flights and falls and wars on the bars).
But the damp doesn't faze us: you adore your dangerous
horse, and the mournful Steve Reich sound its swinging
makes in its endless rise and fall
is the forever music of this moment.

I love the view I get from here,
not just you in your gaiety,
but the whole harbor: Wall Street, Governor's Island,
the Statue in her scaffolding, the halls of Ellis Island,
the spires and towers and bridges of Jersey.
The water today is corrugated cardboard,
just that gray, the same gray as the sky.
Four cargo ships are docked below us,
beyond the runners who keep passing
alone or in pairs, not seeming to notice the scene
or that they're part of it;
there are mysterious boxes—sidecars?—on one deck,
maybe twice my height, although the scale
is hard to tell from here (there are no people),
and rows of toy trucks and barrels on another.
At least three kinds of conveyances
are going about their business in the harbor.
The biggest are the yellow-orange

ferries for Staten Island: one has just pulled
into the copper-green housing that seems to lead
to the hell under Manhattan. The less frequent white
Coast Guard ferries for Governor's Island
seem to crisscross the others' path,
and the red-and-white Circle Line tour boats
look almost too small for what they do,
which is to trudge forever around the big island.
And somewhere out there, too,
are the ones for the Statue,
threading among the unscheduled barges and tugs,
sailboats, tankers, and liners.
All these Sunday conveyances on their regular errands
(not to mention the several machines in the sky)
plying their trade in one big, busy room!
Who could take in everything they've seen:
the smugglings, mutinies, battles, embraces,
fires and flotillas,
yet they all keep soldiering (sailoring) on, as if life were only
this slipping away from the dock and making off
to the destination defined by their speed and capacity.
I say, hats off to their tenacity,
not to mention their color and verve,
that belie their gray surroundings.
Hats off to the jaunty parade they make of their work,
the Sunday painter's curlicues of smoke
twirling up from their stacks, the vestigial
life preservers on their blunted prows,
the proud way they progress in spite of their heft,
these old undaunted harbor dowagers.
Or maybe they're new like you and don't make do
but can only be what they feel.
Nothing stops you either, not choppy water,
silence, or solitude.
You forge ahead like them, your laughter flying
in the face of the uncertain weather and my mood.
Your life is motion,
you can't imagine falling or failing.
You keep on sailing while I push,

the swing sings, and a gentle rain
keeps not quite darkening the ground;
Sunday continues, and another ferry
leaves for another run around.

Brooklyn Aubade

2000

The apartment's snake plants go up
In their placid, green flames,
While the sun, now hitting its stride
Over the unused Navy Yard, amasses
Lit properties from here
To the Trade Towers. The easy-to-catch
Industrial stacks flare first,
Their grey and black-lipped columns,
Buffed to the shine of military
Shoes, trip the first rays
And are taken. Next come the platform
Cranes, little white and red houses
On stilts over the water, their booms
Angled like early fishing rods
Caught in a net of light,
Then a Manhattan glass building
Whose green side turns to red
Or orange on a good morning,
Like a leaf through all its seasons
In an hour, or an otherwise listless mate
Whose chronic jealousy is incited
By the sun's daily overture
To Brooklyn.
Eventually, the Navy Yard's three-
Block-long, mildly blue hangar
(Was this for storing tankers?) is lit,
And the chorus of buildings behind it,
And the municipal stockyard in front—
The fire trucks, police vans and
Garbage trucks—all are collected.
Last comes the half-sunken pier
Where gulls circle and dip down
Like raised dust falling
And rising. The only action in the yard
Is the round of mediations

On what half exists. I remember
My last trip to Houston,
How we drove to the hotel,
Where the hotel used to be,
Where now stands the evacuated shell
Without towels, beds, lamps
Or curtains that a guest might draw
Against the relentless sun,
And we were never in those rooms
But we came almost every day
To the adjoining "Largest Outdoor
Hotel Pool." Padding in sandals,
Unbearably hot, squinting,
We watched them hoist
The building onto trucks,
The liquidating company's brochures
In the display windows where
Brooches used to be.
When we visited last month,
Recounting the tricks we played
To get in, and how we outlived
Those summers by sitting with our friends
And your children by the water,
We pushed up against the gate
And could just make out
The empty pool and the police
Sawhorses around it. Although
We have been forbidden
A certain continuation of the past
—Though I have forbidden this myself
By moving next to the Navy Yard—
The span and reach of your
Goodness moves with me,
Traveling every morning with your
Long strides, while gathering each tall
Memory, each reflective monument,
Any material we could use to fashion
A metropolis of water, metal,
Mercy, and the illuminating
Green flames of love.

Brooklyn Bridge the Other Way
2000

I am walking over the bridge
wrong way, right time.
All the tourists walk toward Manhattan,
guidebooks in hand, to see the skyline.
Yes, *fraulein,* I'd be happy to take
a picture of you all together
then dash off with your Hasselblad
but I'm too old and slow for that daydream
so I just walk broken-field through
the hand-holders and wild bicycles
never looking back at the city
just the dock and clocks of Brooklyn
the Jehovah's Witnesses' digital insistence,
the clock in the warehouse tower
that shouldn't run but does,
the silly Victorian clock on top
of the classical Borough Hall,
a nice payday for some old mayor's brother.
Everyone in Brooklyn carries
an invisible lunch pail.
I bought this bridge a long time ago
and now I'm almost home.

DONALD LEV

Over Brighton

2000

they're repairing the ancient boardwalk
they have a portion of it blocked off
and carpenters are quite busy.
the rest of it is tramped by the many
varieties of humanity.
some skating or cycling, some jogging, most
gossiping, all enjoying God's vast blue skies.
i sit facing the sand facing the sea
in no better repair, certainly
and host to less variety
oh! And then there was the moon.
let's not forget the moon
that had begun rising like some sad and beautiful
warning out of Egypt.

Enemies of Time
2000

"Personally, I
Loved Joe Stalin,"
She murmured into her third martini.

"Love *is* pain."

"Another thirty, forty years . . . it'll all be over."
Said by a bartender in Sunnyside Queens,
Circa 1954.

Me, I love to kill time.
God is going to hate me.

You are the enemy of time,
He'll say.
What can I say?

It's time, old man
    It's time
Your belly hairs
    Are turning white
It's time, old man
    It's time.

As time fades away
The young man hangs around Sheepshead Bay
Making his mother miserable
With his dyed hair
His attitude
His drag.
In a more merciful time
He would have been able to afford his own pad.
In a less merciful time he'd have had to.

#39
2000

"Campy was the hardest man I ever met,"
Kahn the sportswriter said.

Campy, the guinea-nigger-halfbreed,
Kneeling in a Germantown sandlot
With bruised ribs and a ball in his glove.

Campy rising at 1 a.m. to deliver milk
And two blocks' worth of papers.
Campy who had three grown men pull up

In a white Caddy convertible,
Pay his momma three times
Daddy's weekly wage to let him

Catch games on the weekends.
Campy who quit school at 15. Spent ten
Years squatting in the Negro leagues,

Birmingham to Harlem. Spent ten winters
In the Latin leagues—Mexico,
Puerto Rico, Venezuela—making the year

A hard and dusty perpetual summer.
Campy who got the call from Mr. Rickey
To be fourth, join Robinson at Ebbets.

Campy who slept across town
While the rest laughed it up
And danced a block from the stadium.

Campy who got MVP in '51, '53 and '55.
Campy who had mitts so sore he couldn't
Lift the trophy. Who sat upside-down

In an icy car in a Long Island ditch
Thinking how he couldn't feel his legs.
Who sat upstairs, looking out the window

While his wife made love to another man
In the front seat of a Pontiac.
And Campy who grew old remembering

A September afternoon. And that sound.
And how the ball rose steadily
Just inside the third base line

And how he thought,
"Jesus, sweet Lord Jesus, oh it's good to be alive."

ED BARRETT

The Living End
2001

Who are we to forget so much?
>WILLIAM CORBETT

I remember
>JOE BRAINARD

I forget the name of my fifth-grade true love who Danny Abel
with the harelip also liked.

I forget the last four digits of the telephone number we had
when I was growing up on 261—14th Street in Brooklyn which
began Hyacinth 9-. I thought it was the best telephone number
in the whole world.

I forget when the phone company switched from names of
things to numbers for telephone exchanges.

I forget the name of the assistant principal of Bishop Ford High
School. One day he took over Brother Francis's religion class to
give us sex education. He said he'd answer any question we wrote
down anonymously on index cards. We wrote the dirtiest things
we could imagine just to hear him read them out loud because his
face, which was always a cartoon-color red, turned purple when
he was agitated. To the question "What is a blow job?" he an-
swered "When you put your penis in someone's mouth—and
who would want to do such a disgusting thing?" Brother Timo-
thy was the principal, and it bothered me that he had such a
"weak" sounding name.

I forget the name of the boy who sat in front of me in Brother
Francis's religion class. He played bassoon in the school band and
was very shy and one day he was sitting at his desk just staring
down at his religion book when the boy who sat in front of him
was acting up. Brother Francis walked over to our aisle to smack
the kid who was misbehaving, but he hit the bassoon player by

mistake. This shy boy must have been hurt, but he was so surprised by this attack that he just stared up, open-mouthed, at Brother Francis who said "I'm sorry" and then—and this really cracked us up—never hit the kid who was causing the trouble. Brother Francis had a deep, low voice and his head was as big and bald as Elmer Fudd's and we called him Taras Bulba, not after the movie but because his head looked like a light bulb.

I forget the name of the rock band I managed in high school because I couldn't play an instrument or even sing, but I wanted to be part of the scene. Freddie Argenziano on drums, Joe and Charlie Legato on rhythm and base guitar, Steve Carlozzi lead guitar, John Colantoni voice, Bob Palmieri electric keyboard. We played at a happening directed by our drama teacher who later died of AIDS.

I forget when "happenings" stopped.

I forget, now and then, that Theresa is my mother's middle name until I see her sign a check *Beatrice Theresa Barrett*. Her doctor's office receptionist is a black woman from Jamaica who pronounces my mother's first name "Ba-treece," and I like to think of my mother being rechristened at the end of her life with a new name and a new ethnicity.

I forget if I ever thought I wouldn't die. I think I did think that, but I was afraid that everyone else would and I'd be left all alone.

I forget—and this would be sometime later—when I realized the world is just the way I would have wanted it to be, except for the really bad things that can happen, but I'm lucky in my friends and look how beautiful some people are.

I forget the name of one of my swim coaches in grammar school who always showed up late to practice on Thursday evenings at John Jay High School where once a young black girl stood on a third-story ledge and threatened to kill herself and the crowd below chanted *Jump jump,* which made it into *The Daily News* the next day. My nickname on the swim team was Splash. The other coach, Eddie Smith, had a scar from a knife attack from his ear to his mouth.

He went to St. Augustine's which had the coolest purple school jacket.

When I was five, I forget what I said to convince Janie Farrell to step over me as I lay on the ground in the courtyard behind our apartment building so I could look up her dress. I think I just asked her to do it and she thought it was a good idea too.

I really am surprised that I can't think of many more names of the kids I went to Holy Family Grammar School with. Danny Abel, Doreen Gogarty, Michael Matthews, Joeseph Cusamano, Lewis Livesey. Elaine who shared a desk with me and peed her uniform in the afternoon. The name of the boy who had a nose bleed when we stood up for afternoon prayers and a huge booger was dangling from one nostril so he turned around to share this with all of us in his row, hopping from one foot to the other until Sister Kevin Therese slapped him on the side of his head and the booger went flying into the next row of children. We wanted to laugh, but she smacked him really hard so we stood even more rigidly and recited the next *Hail Mary*.

I forget the words to the lullaby my father made up which began *ritchie ritchie roona*. . . .

I forget when Patrick Barrett, who came over from Ireland erected the family headstone in Holy Cross Cemetery. 1838 or 1878. Over dinner recently at a Korean restaurant my mother suddenly announced that she wanted to be cremated. Bibimbop, chicken teriyaki, fish stew and extra kimchee all around.

I have two middle names (Charles William) and I forget who the Charles is I was named after.

I forget what the comic said when five of us went to the Country Club on 7th Avenue in Brooklyn the night we graduated from high school. We wore tuxedo jackets and I had my National

Honor Society medal draped around my neck. Our chapter was named after the medieval scholar Duns Scotus, which we changed to Dumb Scrotum. The comic saw us walk in all dressed up and I think he said "Here come the virgin pimps." His act was mainly insults, and every now and then he'd whip "it" out, made of rubber a foot long and connected to a container of water in his pants which he sprayed over the audience and we all shrank back because even though we knew better it still felt like pee. I forget how long we stayed, but we left feeling like we had enjoyed the show which was packed even though it was an ordinary Wednesday night. Two of us went on to college, two went into the Marines and one was thrown out for being gay. I forget who the fifth boy was. I can't even picture him sitting at our table, laughing with the rest of us.

LISA JARNOT

Brooklyn Anchorage

2001

and at noon I will fall in love
and nothing will have meaning
except for the brownness of
the sky, and tradition, and water
and in the water off the railway
in New Haven all the lights
go on across the sun, and for
millennia those who kiss fall into
hospitals, riding trains, wearing
black shoes, pursued by those
they love, the Chinese in the armies
with the shiny sound of Johnny Cash,
and in my plan to be myself
I became someone else with
soft lips and a secret life,
and I left, from an airport,
in tradition of the water
on the plains, until the train
started moving and yesterday
it seemed true that suddenly
inside of the newspaper
there was a powerline and
my heart stopped, and everything
leaned down from the sky to kill me
and now the cattails sing.

JOSHUA BECKMAN

From Something I Expected to Be Different
2001

It's cold. It's cold. Sky over Brooklyn
don't rain, I have plans for my city today.
Make important promises to me. Lasting.
For not collapse inevitable. Declarations
of foresight on me bestow with continuity
in your nature. Brooklyn sky, has anyone
told you you're all I've got and you
just well up and cry cold Brooklyn rain
over everyone. Sky above Brooklyn I want
promises. I desire promises from individuals
strained to make such promises. Brooklyn cold
my smoke-filled chest buoys up in your waters.
To the extent we can fear the giant fears
coming to pass, I have feared them recently
and today's Brooklyn cold continued on
walking the streets toward the end
of the daytime, enjoying what you said
and your rare appearance departing.

Brooklyn Sestina: June, 1975
2001

How can I conjure the vividness of the plastic
Blue and orange chairs we'd slump
Into every morning before the tyranny of fractions,
Each afternoon after the sadism of lunch?
We'd just played "Boys against Girls,"
"Girls against Boys," slamming each other's small bodies

Into a schoolyard fence, as if to add to the body
Of what American Feminism had become, its piles of plastic
Dolls dismembered like Bluebeard's wives, only this time by girls
Of single mothers slumped
Into plaid couches, too tired or too drunk to fix those cleanly
        cut-out lunches
Like the ones beamed into their living rooms through the Cyclo-
        pean fractal

Blue-rimmed eye of the cathode ray refracted
By those radio ballads that sent everybody
Who'd ever broken up to sobbing in their McDonald's Muzak
        lunches.
Why is it that everything smelled like plastic
As the yellow heatwave slumped
Against my salmon-colored building where the girls

Were jumping rope (the older girls
Skipping double Dutch)? Could it have been the fractious
Yentas looking on from sweaty beach chairs clumped
Together in the shade, their widowed bodies
Already melted and annealed to a tanned and cracking plastic?
The housewives who went on serving each other lunch

Like it would never end? I would soon be off to lunch
Myself at Jewish camp with a girl
My age named Rachel, offering her what I'd plastic-

Wrapped the night before, her six-year-old fractions
Of hands fumbling over my body
In return before our midday swim. No Cold War, no economic
     slump

Could touch us in that Brooklyn; Brooklyn, the word itself seems
     holy,
  a Cabalistic lunchbox
Yawning open for all the world to fathom its great plastic
Letters stretched bodiless
Across the level see-saw of the summer heat like the broken bal-
     loon of a girl's
Insides, her future a fractal-
Patterned leaf dangling from her family tree of dusty plastic.

And the shoulders on the bodies of the girls
Who hadn't been pinned to their beds at night slumped in the
     lunchroom
Nonetheless, its fractured spoons and forks still scattered across
   the dancefloor of my dreams, a threnody of plastic.

Bushwick: Latex Flat

2001

Sadness of just-painted rooms.
We clean our tools
meticulously, as if currying horses:
the little nervous sash brush
to be combed and primped,
the fat old four-inchers
that lap up space
to be wrapped and groomed,
the ceiling rollers,
the little pencils
that cover nailheads
with oak gloss,
to be counted and packed:
camped on our dropsheets
we stare across gleaming floors
at the door and beyond it
the old city full of old rumors
of conspiracies, gunshots, market crashes:
with a little mallet
we tap our lids closed,
holding our breath, holding our lives
in suspension for a moment:
an extra drop will ruin everything.

Minnie & Barbara

2001

Minnie was Aunt Barb's best friend and lived behind her shop—
"Minnie's Beauty Parlour" (spelled the English way to be some-
thing special)—beneath the Metropolitan Avenue El with her
brother, who was "simple" and never held a job other than
sweeping up hair and doing other helpful things in the Beauty
Parlour.

Barbara was unmarried and lived with us in the cold attic bed-
room with my grandmother; if I say she was a seamstress you
possibly wouldn't believe me, since seamstresses exist only in
fairy tales about poor people. But she was. She took the subway
every day to Manhattan, where she worked at Brooks Brothers
upstairs making alterations. This was when Brooks Brothers still
had only one store, on Madison Avenue, and was a place where
only "swells" could buy clothes. A great many ladies did alter-
ations upstairs, all of them very proud—Aunt Barb said—of how
fine a stitch they could sew, of how many stitches to an inch. Her
favorite story was how once, during World War II, she altered a
uniform for General Patton, all of whose uniforms were custom
made.

Every Sunday Minnie and Barbara went to a movie and got din-
ner at a cheap restaurant (Minnie's brother got dinner from the
old lady who lived above Minnie's Beauty Parlour) and then went
home to get a good night's sleep before the work week. The one
story everyone in the family always tells about Barbara is how, in
her seventies, she had gone to a new doctor for a checkup and he
had said in the hearing of my Aunt Carrie, who had taken her,
"Ah, I see that you are still a virgin."

Aunt Carrie roared whenever she told that story, and she told it
often in Barbara's presence, to watch her grow beet-red as she
had, Carrie said, in the doctor's office. Barbara liked to go to the
movies, and Minnie liked them, too, particularly scary ones, and I

remember once in the early fifties they'd gone to see *The Thing* and afterward went to the Chinese restaurant—Aunt Barb and Minnie called it "The Chink's"—above the Ridgewood Movie Theater: she said the movie was scary, so scary they were almost afraid to walk out into the late afternoon sunlight and upstairs for their weekly chow mein, so scary they left The Chink's early so they wouldn't have to walk home from the trolley stop in the dark. "Really, " she told me, "the scariest thing I've ever seen."

A Garbage Can in Brooklyn Full of Books
2001

Schweitzer, *The Teaching of Reverence for Life*.
Tich Nhat Hanh, *The Miracle of Mindfulness*.
Mortimer Adler, *Ten Philosophical Mistakes*.
John Stuart Mill in the familiar
formal attire of a Penguin Classic.
A few with *psychoanalysis* in the titles.

I see how it might get tiresome to have such titles
imploring you day after day to change your life.
It could easily plunge you into the classic
cycle of guilt and self-improvement, mindfulness
followed by depression, each glance at those familiar
spines reminding you of all the mistakes

you've made in the past, and the mistakes
to come. Who wouldn't want to clear the titles
from the shelves and return to the familiar
routine of a comfortable life
undisturbed by thought? A blissful mindlessness.
Throw away every last unread classic

(there's no such thing as a classic
anyway, they now say). Look, the whole mess takes
up only one can, though to undeniable fullness.
But wait. Digging down, I find the serious titles
have risen to the top like cream, or like the life-
preservers they're supposed to be (familiar

wisdom hauling us back up to the familiar
from uncertain depths). Or else these classics
have been placed on top deliberately, as if life
depended on concealing our . . . mistakes?
No, just dozens of trash novels flaunting bold titles
and heroines with breasts of unreal fullness—

like the fantasies our minds are full of,
hidden by good intentions—sound familiar?
What is this bizarre collection of titles
(quasi-porno side by side with classics)
but the unfinished, bound-to-be-full-of-mistakes
bibliography of someone's inner life?

From "The World at Night"

2001

I went out one night with people from work
to an editor's apartment. I drank
a glass of poison. She served me poison
and everyone else was either immune
or politely refused. In the subway
I didn't know the meanings of any words
and my sweat stung me. People on the car
pushed me off at the next stop when I puked
in my hands. Without any meaning, time
accreted to things in funny shapes—old,
asymmetrical hobbledehoys
tormented me, a stern but benevolent
lizard gave me counsel. My stomach contents
spilled around me. My mind was actually
seven or eight minds, all but one of them
composed of helicopters. The other one
was sad. Satellites could tell I was sad.
When another subway came I crawled on
and technically I passed into death, but
passed through and awoke at Coney Island
and saw black cowboys galloping on the beach.
Hungry, mentally defeated, I stared
at the World's Largest Rat—for fifty cents.
Really, it was only the same color
as a rat. "It's from the same family,"
the barker explained. I felt vulnerable
illuminated by neon and fried light.
Everyone had to use one big toilet
and the sky was orange with satellites.
And satellites know everything.

Bones

2002

(*after Hart Crane*)

"I, too, was liege / To rainbows currying" pulsant bones.
The "sun took step of" Brooklyn Bridge's resonant bones.

From Far Rockaway to Golden Gate I saw blood
washed up on streets against God's irrelevant bones.

If the soul were a body, what would it insist on?
On smooth skin? On stubborn flesh? Or on elegant bones?

"The window goes blond slowly." And I beside you
am stripped and stripped and stripped to luxuriant bones.

So Elizabeth had two hundred Catholics burned
(Bloody Mary had loved the smoke of Protestant bones).

In the hair of Pocahontas a forest shudders.
Inventions cobblestone her extravagant bones.

They refuse to burn when we set fire to the flesh—
those flowers float down the Ganges as adamant bones.

"Footprints on the Glacier" are the snowman's—or mine?
Whosever, they're found under some hesitant bones.

Someone once told us he had lost his pity for
(he did not qualify with "ignorant" or "tolerant") bones.

Migrating from me to me to me the soul asks
a bit seriously: what is our covenant, Bones?

Mustard oil, when heated, breaks out in veins which then
cayenne the sacrificed goat's most compliant bones.

The troops left our haven hanging in the night and said
The child's skeleton was made of militant bones.

And so it was Shahid entered the broken world
when everyone had bypassed the heart's expectant bones.

The Wilson Avenue Kings
2002

A child with glittering eyes
spat on me, slashed my jacket
with his box cutter

and now the cop holding him
in a hammerlock ordered:
hit as hard as you want.

Snow drifted in whorls
in the arc of a high lamp.
A dog's silhouette paced
behind a frosted window.

As I backed away
trying to make each step slower
eyes in hallways
picked up my trembling.

Each door was covered
with one stroke of a letter
of an immense name

and the cop shouted after me:
Faggot. I risked my life.

L. S. ASEKOFF

The Widows of Gravesend
2002

It is told & it is told & it is told again.
Whispered in the kitchen by women
dividing violets,
separating beans from stones.
There came a man then
walking in his father's shoes
who heard the three dogs barking by the stream
& at the crossroads
owned neither by this woman nor that man
saw two white horses in a line
& said, "Yes, I am a wanderer in my own land."

Who are you anyway?
An old crow fallen among gold apples?
A man shaving his father's face in the mirror?
Naked under the white sow of the moon
with only the fakebook of Beauty for feeling,
you think, *What is my life?*
A dog abandoned at the end of summer?
A walk in the rain?
I have lived with my body so long, is it not my soul?

Sadness tunes the instrument.
There is a chill on everything.
You feel the surge, the violent momentum of
emptiness filling immense forms,
energy frozen in each cell,
the snowplow in a white sea of waves spellbound by starlight.

Night, night,
sweetest sister,
weary river flowing on,
who will sing all our tomorrows?
The lucky ones who continue to live having nothing?

In Brooklyn
2002

I would engage in an argument with him
then go near to dedication of a poem to him.
Bring me with you then go again I ask, fright,
Listen to me. Listen lovers
in movies who never made it
to the top of the Empire State Building, and that lovers
who never established an intimacy could make a female poet
and not a male poet though I do grow body parts
things gone then meadows

O

This is out of control enter
magical goat-herder over yon river
comes little boy/mommy. Gosh this
is it, the place known, bucolic
longing and for nothing. For little men
not up in spaceships but here in my bedroom at night and
is no one awake for me—no one to save me and
green/pink bright lustiness flung out at stars
falls to speakers who crow (mercy mercy)

O

Energetic half a mortal lifetime allowed. Command
for the truth is that skies as done masturbate lubed up 'gan slosh-
        ing—
O arthritis in the stars signals messengers to flee flee
and no rhythms to it, nothing to it but quick snaps and wings
on feet. Strange in bed. Talked of a lot and beaten into their
        heads
that there is a deformity. It brings out my sympathy.
It is sad.

O

Generally thinking of lines (guilt) conventional
passengers everyone was on the subway today and I
thought of an essay on sin, on the seven deadly sins
and how one could never once do or be anything but this—
and eternity faced it this generally thinking of lines (guilt)
and passing the time not well not
doing much or not working hard either gist
pay attention and I will do lots to get you to
look at me and to think of me, talk of me.

MARILYN HACKER

Elegy for a Soldier
2002

June Jordan 1936—2002

I

The city where I knew you was swift.
A lover cabbed to Brooklyn
(broke, but so what) after the night shift
in a Second Avenue
diner. The lover was a Quaker,
a poet, an anti-war
activist. Was blonde, was twenty-four.
Wet snow fell on the access
road to the Manhattan Bridge. I was
neither lover, slept uptown.
But the arteries, streetlights, headlines,
phonelines, feminine plural
links ran silver through the night city
as dawn and the yellow cab
passed on the frost-blurred bridge, headed for
that day's last or first coffee.

The city where I knew you was rich
in bookshops, potlucks, ad hoc
debates, demos, parades and picnics.
There were walks I liked to take.
I was on good terms with two rivers.
You turned, burned, flame-wheel of words
lighting the page, good neighbor on your
homely street in Park Slope, whose
Russian zaydes, Jamaican grocers,
dyke vegetarians, young
gifted everyone, claimed some changes
—at least a new food co-op.
In the laundromat, ordinary

women talked revolution.
We knew we wouldn't live forever
but it seemed as if we could.

The city where I knew you was yours
and mine by birthright: Harlem,
the Bronx. Separately we left it
and came separately back.
There's no afterlife for dialogue,
divergences we never
teased apart to weave back together.
Death slams down in the midst of
all your unfinished conversations.
Whom do I address when I
address you, larger than life as you
always were, not alive now?
Words are not you, poems are not you,
ashes on the Pacific
tide, you least of all. I talk to my-
self to keep the line open.

The city where I knew you is gone.
Pink icing roses spelled out
PASSION on a book-shaped chocolate cake.
The bookshop's a sushi bar
now, and PASSION is long out of print.
Would you know the changed street that
cab swerved down toward you though cold white mist?
We have a Republican
mayor. Threats keep citizens in line:
anthrax; suicide attacks.
A scar festers where towers once were;
dissent festers unexpressed.
You are dead of a woman's disease.
Who gets to choose what battle
takes her down? Down to the ocean, friends
mourn you, with no time to mourn.

You, who stood alone in the tall bay window
of a Brooklyn brownstone, conjuring morning
with free-flying words, knew the power, terror
in words, in flying;

knew the high of solitude while the early
light prowled Seventh Avenue, lupine hungry
like you, your spoils raisins and almonds, ballpoint
pen, yellow foolscap.

You, who stood alone in your courage, never
hesitant to underline the connections
(between rape, exclusion and occupation . . .)
and separations
were alone and were not alone when morning

blotted the last spark of you out, around you
voices you no longer had voices to answer,
eyes you were blind to.

All your loves were singular: you scorned labels.
Claimed *black; woman,* and for the rest eluded
limits, quicksilver (Caribbean), staked out
self-definition.

Now your death, as if it were "yours" : your house, your
dog, your friends, your son, your serial lovers.
Death's not "yours," what's yours are a thousand poems
alive on paper,

in the present tense of a thousand students'
active gaze at printed pages and blank ones
which you gave permission to blacken into
outrage and passion.

You, at once an optimist, a Cassandra,
Lilith in the wilderness of her lyric,

were a black American, born in Harlem,
citizen soldier.

If you had to die—and I don't admit it—
who dared "What if, each time they kill a black man /
we kill a cop?" couldn't you take down with you
a few prime villains

in the capitol, who are also mortal?
June, you should be living, the states are bleeding.
Leaden words like "Homeland" translate abandoned
dissident discourse.

Twenty years ago, you denounced the war crimes
still in progress now, as Jenin, Ramallah
dominate, then disappear from the headlines.
Palestine: your war.

"To each nation, its Jews," wrote Primo Levi.
"Palestinians are Jews to Israelis."
Afterwards, he died in despair, or so we
infer, despairing.

To each nation, its Jews, its blacks its Arabs,
Palestinians, immigrants, its women.
From each nation its poets: Mahmoud Darwish,
Kavanagh, Shahid

(who, beloved witness for silenced Kashmir,
cautioned, shift the accent, and he was "martyr"),
Audre Lourde, Neruda, Amichai, Senghor,
and you, June Jordan.

Jack Roosevelt

2002
"You will never know how easy it was for me
because of Jackie Robinson."
MARTIN LUTHER KING, JR.

1920

Mama and Edgar,
Frank, Mack, Willa Mae, Jackie
all clacking on the tracks in the COLOREDS ONLY car
out to California from Georgia where Papa done snuck out,
gone, end of story. Or beginning,
stuffed in a shack with aunt, uncle, cousins while
day in, out, Mama's knees splintery, scabbing
all for pocket change, table scraps, hand-me-downs
for Edgar, Frank, Mack, Willa Mae, Jackie.
It's the wantin' that keeps ya movin,' liftin,' lovin'
the hope in work, those stretched limbs a' loyalty
gone limp come nighttime
into the dark, dark cool of rest.

1924

Edgar, Frank, Mack, Willa Mae, but Jackie too young
for school, for home with Mama
scrubbing, scouring, too far away to be there.
It's the work that gives ya pride, that keeps ya movin'
till Willa Mae's teacher sighed, *OK, Jackie, sit,*
sit, outside my window, still as home plate
in that square pit of sand,
but come in, come in
when it rains.

1928

Two meals, one, maybe none but Robinson
walls, roof, floor, good enough to scrub, to pray on

and Edgar, Frank, Mack, Willa Mae, Jackie
all clacking up down up down stairs onto
a porch wide as two cleaned-out closets but cool
so cool in the hot hot heat of the day.

1928

And across their own their own
their own street from a girl not eight
and a father with aim enough to pitch
stones and "nigger, nigger, nigger" names. *Shame, shame*
said the white lady across their own
their own street *for fighting with a child,*
a little child, as she tugged her husband,
her child, back
into the white
dirty house.

1936

Then Mack clacking along the olympic track,
eyeing silver just back of Jesse;
Jackie home smacking balls on bats,
balls in nets, over nets, over goal posts, over goalies,
till kids, coaches, parents, reporters turned,
Hey, hey boy, you'se good. You'se real good!
and others turned quicker than *wha'the?*
and spit a clean shot. It's the biting of the lip
that chews you up, spews you out
sometimes sour, sometimes spent,
sometimes strong enough
to keep the wood cracking,
the leather bashing
past the plate,
and get you home.

1945

Student, lieutenant, then a short
stop in Kansas City, a Monarch,
black as every other
but paid to play. What could be better
when the gates smack shut
to the wrong skin
from the wrong
side of the tracks?

1945–62

Till the Dodgers dodged
moans, groans, clean shots
of spit from their "fans" as Branch Rickey
sharpened his pencil, his tongue: *This
is what to do* and Robinson sharpened
his swing, his spirit: *This is
what to do* and cracked the chain
gates, the monochrome stands, to linedrive
the smudged-as-a-baseball rules up,
past the park, past the tracks,
across the country, and home
into the Hall of Fame.

1972

And it's cool so cool
in the hot hot heat of the day
when the ball soars where you put it,
when the wood
clacks out your name.

Train to Coney Island
2003

This time I'm going all the way to the Mermaid Parade, I only
    wish
I were a photographer! It's late, I hope the floats won't be
    dismantled.
Last night I dreamt that L. and I got married but our audience
was not behaving—Jennifer Miller the bearded lady kept yap-
    ping. In real life
I splintered up and asked M. for a second chance: "I'll
    change," etc.
We are all equally deceived, perhaps, by ourselves. One thing I
    know for sure:
it's pointless to hope I have an encyclopedic mind. All it ever
    retains
is the bare-bones sentiment of the thing, the hiss of information
rushing off into the canyon. I don't really mind, words chip off
    the block
and float in summer air. They're nothing compared to the but-
    tery rings
of Saturn! & I have always been a sucker for mystification. Here
    we are
at Neptune Avenue! It's funny and a little sad that I've written
    such a chatty,
prosy sonnet, as all I wanted was to take the train to its final
    destination
and write a teeny chiseled poem, some perfect illumination.

Coca-Cola and Coco Frio

2003

On his first visit to Puerto Rico,
island of family folklore,
the fat boy wandered
from table to table
with his mouth open.
At every table, some great-aunt
would steer him with cool spotted hands
to a glass of Coca-Cola.
One even sang to him, in all the English
she could remember, a Coca-Cola jingle
from the forties. He drank obediently, though
he was bored with this potion, familiar
from soda fountains in Brooklyn.

Then, at a roadside stand off the beach, the fat boy
opened his mouth to coco frio, a coconut
chilled, then scalped by a machete
so that a straw could inhale the clear milk.
The boy tilted the green shell overhead
and drooled coconut milk down his chin;
suddenly, Puerto Rico was not Coca-Cola
or Brooklyn, and neither was he.

For years afterward, the boy marveled at an island
where the people drank Coca-Cola
and sang jingles from World War II
in a language they did not speak,
while so many coconuts in the trees
sagged heavy with milk, swollen
and unsuckled.

TOM SLEIGH

From Brooklyn Bridge
(*from "New York American Spell," 2001*)
2003

Sun shines on the third bridge tower:
A garbage scow ploughs the water,

Maternal hull pushing it all out beyond
The city, pushing it all out so patiently—

All you could hear out there this flawless afternoon
Is the sound of sand pulverizing newsprint

To tatters, paper-pulp ripping crosswise
Or lengthwise, shearing off some photo

Of maybe a head or maybe an arm.
Ridiculous flimsy noble newspaper,

Leaping in wind, fluttering, collapsing,
Its columns sway and topple into babble:

All you'd see if you were out there
Is air vanishing into clearer air.

ANNE PIERSON WIESE

Last Night in Brooklyn

2004

There is a sheen of traffic noise
on the expressway—not a sound so much
as the absence of sleep. Dutch
settlers with their staffs, Van Brunt and Van Nuyse,

ended journeys and began, pancake blue hats poised
to slip from their heads into the wan dust
of coast roads like maps, followed their wanderlust
here, tracks of salt, cheese rinds tossed to porpoises

in the bay, arriving fires in the damp
night, scrounging the ground for good flat rocks,
leaving metal, bones, broken bits, fine china, hoists
of rope cached deep below these cement ramps'
unpresent hum. 3 AM. The digital clock
glows. Out my window clings the moon—mum as an oyster.

Ailanthus

2004

In their distorting internal mirrors,
the battered and in pain
become the dragons mauling them.
Their spirits drain

to their spleens, which manufacture
a substance, viscous, green
that catalyzes their hearts'
colorless acetylene,

igniting their dragon breath.
Then they breathe and burn.
The ones who did them dirt
are done to in turn.

The ones who stopped to watch
are torched to black pathetic stems
by holographic Greek fire
and ICBMs.

And what happens to
those servants of the state
whose fault it all is is too
painful to relate.

Brothers and sisters to dragons!—
but only in their dreams
the mountain spews,
the fissure streams.

Elsewhere the tree-of-heaven grows—
in deserted parking lots,
auto graveyards, abandoned
garden plots.

The wind in its leaves
is dry, arrhythmic, and sad.
Everyone, it whispers, has their reasons,
a few of which are bad.

Brooklyn
2004

I didn't know where I was that night.
There was a party on Winthrop Street
and I arrived with my cardboard suitcase
straight from Rochester through Penn Station.

I came by the Q train early afternoon
in my green spring jacket and gold flats
and I was okay, even though I was in Brooklyn
because my friends would meet me and take me home.

And anyway Aunt Chasha lived on that street
and she'd be waiting, looking out around nine
from the window of her egg store
for me to come and stay over with her.

But it turned out the kids I knew didn't show up.
There were weather warnings and they were afraid
the town would be snowed in. So I sat there alone
too scared of strangers to ask what to do.

And took my case and started walking in the dusk
as small flakes began to fall. And I thought
what luck I just have to get to the fourteen hundreds
and I'm safe, Aunt Chasha waiting in the window.

It got dark and the street was empty
and my party shoes stuck in the deepening snow.
I was sneezing and wet, afraid, sixteen
in the street menacing with night and silence.

And the numbers stopped. The street
came to an end and light and humanity
had come to an end and I was not near
Aunt Chasha in the window of her egg store.

Eleven hundred, twelve hundred.
The stores on the corner were all closed
because of the snow. I was cold.
My mother had told me not to go.

Suddenly there was quickening:
A man was cleaning his windshield
just enough to see to drive. Even from far
it was clear he was very drunk.

"It's too hard to explain," when I asked him
where the street had disappeared. "I'll take you."
His car faced the opposite way. I weighed
wandering and pneumonia against certain death

And got in. Drugged by whiskey fumes and fear.
I said nothing as the car reeled
back down the numbers of Winthrop,
skidded right, and right, and again.

A lurch, a screech, the square of light.
Aunt Chasha in the window peering out.
"Such a terrible night! Such a terrible neighborhood."
"It's all right," I said, "My friend's father brought me."

Uncle Dugan
2005

A van knocked down the kid playing tag.
The rest of us stood on a manhole cover
above Brooklyn's slurring waste
and beneath the elevated train

that sawed the sun and moon in two.
The driver waved a fifth
of Four Roses like a bad wand
and we disappeared

while tenements emptied to the curb
where Alice Gallon sang "Chantilly Lace"
until her mother slapped
her face with a sauce spoon

with some tomato sauce still on it.
I went home to parts of a steer
bobbing in broth while Uncle Dugan
exhaling Pall Malls toward

the teardrop chandelier and drinking
Heaven Hill from the bottle.
He said one law demands we eat well
but another keeps food from the poor,

that I was lucky I stayed put
on the iron disk
above Smith Street's suds and shit,
but should know

that even though I'm safe
before a placemat and a spoon,
no drink or art is strong enough
to undermine the fact

that every victim
once inhabited the crowd
of witnesses like you
and you and you.

V. Bridge View
(from "The Narrows")
2005

The grandeur of the tower was nothing at first
but our surmise at what it would become,
gleaned from rumors; though before long
we watched the stanchions' gradual ascent
above Shore Road's distant stand of trees
where Third narrowed to its vanishing point.

Nothing at first, and then, from the corner,
one day we saw the legs barely risen,
two sheer columns of iron and steel:
the tensile things of a man being built
foot by lifted foot from the bottom up,
girder and crossbeam, rivet and plate.

For two years he grew, his height accruing
like a child's stature notched on a wall,
while up from the Narrows the body took form
from foot to hips and vaulted crotch. But where
was the rest of him, broad torso and head?
It was we who gave that image to the air,

gave it likewise its twin across the strait
before they strung the cables, hung the roadway
amazingly into place, so that, that first time,
we drove through a space left by torn-down homes
up the approach, the Island spread before us,
the river below, and climbed into the sky.

A Mosque in Brooklyn

2005

There is no prayer that can abolish history,
though in this basement mosque the muezzin's history

gathers in his throat like a tenor's aria
and he calls to God to put an end to history.

From my courtyard room I hear his song ascending,
the divine name whirling its rebuke to history—

Allah, Allah—above the crowded rowhouse roofs.
Their rusted antennas, stalled arrows of history,

would transmit a daily riot of talk and news,
the world boxed inside a glowing square of history.

I've seen them on the street, the faithful in their robes
walking along store-fronts, a different history

clothing them, like me, in our separate skins,
though here we are at the scope-end of history:

Goodness is timeless, the great English poet wrote,
and not just for himself—the crime is history.

But as if to prove the old Sufi fable true
these prayers are lifted on the thermals of history,

and sound strangely like that congregation of birds;
no, the remnant who survived a blighted history,

having stayed their quest into the final valley
where a Great Tree rose, its branches thick as history.

And there they lost themselves, flourishing into the One
without division, without names, without history.

Swell of Flame

2007

The big man is headed up Degraw in his fireguy uniform, all
    speckled black and neon
yellow for some Saturday morning chow with his boys, Bobbie
    and Frankie,
the Jew from Bayside, Rosenblum, who they used to call *Yid* but
    now
Rosie,

such a hazel light this morning off the brownstone brick
five sirens barrel down Smith and I can't help but wonder
which new tragedy has befallen the city,
some maniac with dynamite on track two at Boro Hall, boom,
all that bent steel, in bed
next to Rachel, mid-dream, almost light blue sky for breakfast,

those red trucks used to make love to me when I was six
and slid them down my smooth floors toward an imaginary blaze
    at the end of the hall,

I wanted to be that big man up my street this morning
in those cool boots,
now just the Dalmatian with a regal coat who sits as mascot for
    all that is quiet,
all that is horror,

haven't we suffered enough in our own banjo cut short dreams?
haven't we heard the blare of those horns at four in the morning
    one too many times?

it makes me wonder how that big man travels up Degraw to fire-
    house 204
near Court each Saturday
and puts his gear in a locker labeled *Chooch,*

it's got to be the same thing that brings us home each evening to
    this swell of flame
up on the black roof and skyward.

Suburbia

2007

Whitman's Brooklyn is a hook, a language
of the lost and found, of pastoral rezones,
of diction, politics, and sycamores.
The boys-gone-men hold sticks and dream of fields.

School-night-weather—the wind is a nudge
and leafskitter hints of somewhere else.
We'll have to drive there, board a bus or train
or something that will move him to the outskirts.

Picture Whitman on a hill as a child, Brooklyn
all smoke and mirrors for a boy with a kite
going quid-pro-quo with the big blue,
kite blocking out the sun, what distracted Adam

from the first miracle as his rib was taken and grew forth.
Could he have imagined big Bill Levitt and his urge to build?
Long Island is a rib grown catastrophic and lovely,
a few arteries and smaller roads, meticulously mapped

capillaries—and towns—the Oyster Bays, the Huntingtons.
It's where Quo finds more than mere ginkgoes;
where the concrete shtetl can go green,
the block and tackle of Balsams and Dogwoods,

a little Hemlock parasol of petals and needles,
and lofty speech a kite for grounded men.
Picture Whitman, old now, a shade in the sun,
his kite over Camden, his mind back to Brooklyn

and out towards towns not rural but far from central.
There's no more either-or: we've got smoke and cloud,
arrival and exodus, and the tethers
that bear us up, keep us here, and suggest flight.

Walking through Prospect Park with Suzan
2007

We hear a sound like a mammoth door
creaking open. She tells me it's a woodpecker,

and I imagine that little nose opening worlds.
I think of hearing a poet read a few weeks ago;

sitting in the front row I wanted nothing more
than to touch his nose. I told this to my friends

at Pete's Tavern after the reading and someone
called it sweet. Jeff would probably call it sublimation.

I start talking with Suzan about how difficult it is
to marry appearances with intention and she wants

to walk around what looks like mint but could be
poison ivy. My mother used to grow mint

in our backyard; we called it by its Arabic name, *nana*.
Only a few years ago I learned the English word

for *tukie* is *mulberries* and *ramane* is *pomegranate*.
I have spent my life confusing words, mixing up

what I mean with what I say. The other day
when we were lying on my kitchen floor and I said

you should go, I could have said *I'm scared*
or *help me believe*. But there is little to believe in

since what we see is not necessarily out there
and language hollows being into desire.

Even when I try to talk about what I want I start to lie.
There's a lot to be said for walking around things.

Still, there are times when a skeptic tries,
a woodpecker banging itself into a tree.

ANDREA BAKER

West Street

2007

Someone's honking jingle bells. A dog's humping a cat on top of a
low tin roof. Someone's dumping a baby stroller the wheels have
fallen off of. People have pulled their cars over to fight. Here I
can walk unnoticed. I can walk without noticing myself. But just
the curious man in a suit is walking a designer dog. And the dog
on the roof. The woman alone in her car crying. The sign some-
one bought and posted saying No Parking or Stranding. As if one
person, through words, could gain control. As if anyone has ever
had a chance against contrary signs bolted to other things. Every-
thing is so terrifying on West Street. The cop van goes by looking
for the criminals. We are all the ones who want to go to heaven.
The woman carrying a pile of papers. The dog peeing in the alley.
The fat man seems to be looking for something. What he finds is
uneven, broken, and covered in skin.

The Million Dollar Poem
or
You Must Change Your Life
2007

said a poem
and for five seconds I considered church attendance and polite
     interest
  in the public health, in a steel-rimmed Baker-Eddy sort of way
as I trod briskly on Atlantic in search of Pacific, trusting
      they would intersect soon, near an All-Pork Halal I had
      read up on
         and I could buy some lunch on the way to
            lunch—Ha! Change My Life? So right then I
        invented this "million dollar poem" poem

for what did *that* poem know about me and mine and how to
     change it, though I knew the
            answer, I knew!

And who do they think they are, those male maidens cooing
     from turrets to lutes
  dishing frilly translations curlicued with good tidings and illu-
     sory pontifications
     in alexandrines and crème de la crème brulée to nibble by
     the sparkling   Manahatta of a summer's eve?

            Every chip-
            shred-chip
            stomp, hay
            foot, straw
            foot foot
            foot foot

        "This side up side down"

on the march to the smothered Gowanus
ekes its toll from my sandals and I won't
    beat gold leaf for the eyeshadows of Hatshepsut's needle
    or tease cymbals from crystal timbrels or shop on Vlietbosc
    for the fabrics—*dash!*—*dash!*—of cashmere to make me
            beautiful (good luck) &c.
for no! I've got to write
    this one million dollar poem!
    Just this one!
    Each day's shift has its special demands

Schedule

Mondays: half-days; Tuesdays : I'm psalmic
    "Let the dogs return to their vomit" a perennial favorite
    fit for every pocketbook, side effects, not, alas paregoric;

        two-for-one love-and-loss Thursdays; the occa-
sional sabbatical   Arabic
        and rhapsodes when I'm in such a mood or my
back
        is up against the dessert rush—all with or with-
out
        your choice of cold beverage
        Wednesdays, Fridays—reader's choice!

Change your life? Buddy! I still haven't got one!
    Who has time . . . I'm dime
    thin and running late from hand-me-down hot dogs like
you
        who went flush on anthologies sold out in Poughkeepsie
and
        Peekskill and the other "P" towns

then sat around museums mumbling *ah! marmora* through-
out Modernism

while I'm Marie de France du jour here in a crinoline apron
serving it up and prince charming Dear Reader just turned
into a bona fide wolf:

something, really, really has got to change
my life.

JONAH WINTER

I'll Have a Manhattan
2007

It was one of those Coney Island dives frequented only by old
    drunks—
you probably know what I'm talking about: there might be a pool
    table
but no one's playing pool; no one's talking—they're all at the bar
playing out the final acts of their own private tragedies,

slumped or propped over a beer and a shot,
maybe talking quietly to themselves, maybe not, but at the very
    least
avoiding lively conversation as they while away the afternoon
in a place that smells a little too much of toilet disinfectant for
    my taste.

I guess I was drawn in by the Christmas decorations:
A Santa Claus revolving in the window,
perhaps in sync with a Mrs. Claus—I can't remember. Whatever
    it was,
it gave me the guts to walk inside, among the silent drunks

who stared at me like I was from a different planet,
sneering as I walked up to the end of the bar and stood there
several minutes, unable to get the attention of the bartender
who looked almost as drunk as his customers

and basically was pretending to be busy while I waited to order
my drink, a gin & tonic, which, when I finally ordered it,
brought about some chuckles, coughing fits, outright laughter
    and mumbled slurs
from the clientele who watched to see how their pal would han-
    dle me.

Perhaps I should mention that I looked quite young,
my hair was sticking up in various directions,

and my arm was in a cast—causing the bleary-eyed barkeep
to look me up and down a couple of times before saying

"I can't serve you," at which point I'd already opened my billfold
to show him my ID, but too late—he'd turned his back again
and this time was outwardly ignoring me.
I tried shouting at him, telling him what he was doing was
         against the law,

but of course to no avail.
I can't remember how I finally got drunk that night.
It was probably snowing outside.
I probably walked through the snow

to the restaurant bar with the glowing fish tanks
and drank Manhattans, closing my eyes
for a long, long time, trying to picture
the deep blue sea just down the street,

entirely and purely loving, some
ocean voyage lit by stars, immersed
in the black Atlantic night . . . , saying *Yeah,*
I think I'll have another one.

DAVID MARGOLIS

Life Is Not Complicated and Hard,
Life Is Simple and Hard
2007

They're always trying to jew you down.
'Take this, it's cheaper.'
Not this Brooklyn boy—
Too smart.

Or else they try to turn you around.
'Take this, it's better.'
But this smart Brooklyn boy's
Too tough.

It's tough and smart you have to be
In this world, boy—you better believe it.
There isn't any in between—
Take it or leave it.

So teach yourself to shop around,
Make sure to learn good quality.
But tough and smart's the easy part:
Perversity.

    Yes, smart and tough
    Is only enough,
    So when you feel
    There's something more,
    And start to deal.
    Make what you sell,
    Be smart and tough
    (But only enough),
    Your door unlocked,
    Your shelves well-stocked.
    Taking as known
    A gift's a loan,
    You'll quite soon see

A loan's a gift.
Prosperity's
The normal drift,
To live at ease
Like dogs and trees.

Volcano on Grand Street
2007

At the end of Grand Street
under the Brooklyn Queens Expressway
that's quiet for American Thanksgiving
the top blows on a local volcano
and everyone down the street
cranes their necks to see

Where did it come from?
Is it a piece from a movie set
   fallen off a quick truck
     on the elevated highway?
Or a bit of low cloud
   moving in from the East River?

Upstairs a black woman on TV laughs and laughs.

Lava pours towards us
I see my reflection, someone
gravely looking

   Everyone stays inside
   everyone looks for something—

Like lovers that lava entwined
we wish to die, to be completed
through catastrophe
through private audience with Shiva
memorized by fire
particulated
ash in clouds
undistinguished, at home,
nothing left to break down—

I want to be on the front lines—
I get ready to go outside—

If I really put my shoes on
if I really walk down to the BQE
if I get close enough to the heat
if I stop at a molten sea
if I jump into the lava and am turned to glass
if as glass I take my true form—
Will I be memorialized
eulogized
make front-page news
be shown on TV?

All over the neighborhood
glass bodies twinkle like Christmas lights
firemen glide by in heat-resistant boots
plucking dog-walkers and fallen babies
from the hardening rock
setting us on the sidewalk
cooling us with hoses
while we view the molten river
that has changed us—

ANTHONY LACAVARO

The Old Italian Neighborhood

2007

That Friday in June, God transubstantiated Fate
into exact change, not for the bus or even the quick
exit from the restaurant, bill complete with tip,

but instead for the perfectly finished evening,
from buying beer and cigarettes to redressing late fees,
as if God understood I was not to blame

for keeping those films, horrible as they were,
my sin more than expiated by watching them in the first place.
A simple song from the dark church towers

in the borough of many churches played me past quiet old men
in white T-shirts who had once believed they were gods.
Such is the beauty that will then empty a sky

on the way home, with a bag bound to rip
before I arrive, full of the unnecessary, except
on a Friday, pockets empty as a sky may be.

From a brownstone's highest windows
so thankfully not ours, I heard the frustration
only a baby can muster, a cry that echoes between the parents,

bouncing off one to the other, intensifying with each
pass, and with each a clear remembrance of the last time
either could turn to the other

in a gesture of desire without exhaustion, without
first tasting salt on the lips before an introductory kiss,
when desire inaugurated every weekend,

when a hand did not lie heavily on the thigh,
when seduction talk did not sound worn and heartless
even when cribbed from a Persian love song.

So quickly I passed to our own, not thankful
for God's gifts, whatever shapes they may have taken,
but that God finally caught up with the age,

that God knew how often late fees drag on,
neighborly cousin to the monthly credit card bill,
that corner shops may keep odd hours in Brooklyn,

leaving one to find candy in the antiquated
and somewhat suspect bubble jars set seemingly
in wrought iron, that redeeming even an hour

may fall simply into a cashier's hands
when he happily takes my last dollar and I am
on my way past brownstones with angry babies,

so many new and angry babies anxious to flood
the morning streets, back to an apartment,
curved and weird as an apartment may be,

but where our own baby has already gone quickly to sleep,
the religious chimes go quiet in our ears
and the taste of salt will only be the taste of salt.

Sunday Café

2007

(*Tea Lounge, Park Slope, Brooklyn*)

Look around this café, everyone is reading the New York Times
    and talking,
which all adds up to a clamor of breakfast noises and a mosaic of
    Sunday papers.
Look at this messy cartoon I call my "life," which does not know
whether it is living or being lived.
It happened again on the way here:
a man looked at me on the subway, directly, meaningfully,
    brazenly.
This is a different way of being a woman,
which I always disdained, complained, refrained from and now
something must cry look at me, look at me!
And the thrill of being looked-at quivers me to attention.
Being noticed, like noticing, has a sharp blade.
I too cannot help but notice all the beautiful women who popu-
    late this restaurant,
it seems they are too beautiful to possibly be real;
and what is it all for anyway, all this ungraspable perfection, be-
    cause
although right now their beauty is as full as a ripe boysenberry,
crushable, staining, straining their own edges, aching
to be popped in the mouth and tasted
(and they offer it as such)
soon it will be over, their beauty, and only the desire will remain.
All the fucking in the world never erases desire,
and moreover it creates a Next Generation with desire of their
    own.
So any cessation of desire becomes futile, impossible.
And so we keep putting on our strappy heels day after day,
just "not feeling right" if we wear sneakers or flip flops,
offering ourselves up for this one day:

offering our beauty on the altar of this particular Sunday
like a coffee and a newspaper, to be swallowed and read
and left behind on the cafe table,
leaving faint black smudges on our one-day-older fingertips.

Jamaica Bay

2007

Only from the air can you see them,
the small islands of ebb and flood.
Ghostlike hills, brown under green water.
Low tide exposes the sand banks.

Kelp grows here, mussels and snails live here.
Sometimes a white heron comes fishing.
No bird will ever spend the night here,
unsafe from the rising tide.

It takes years before reeds can grow
and anchor mud and sand. The island will grow,
become safe, ducks can nest there.
Horse shoe crabs will mate on its sand.

Without humans the bay would be forgotten.
Each island could grow, the land would invade the sea.

But that will never happen. People dredge here.
Big ships must be able to enter the bay.

MELISSA BEATTIE-MOSS

After We Make Love
2007

That's when the news is the worst.
That's when the deaths of others become my death or yours.
That's when the ache in my breast, my left breast
is not benign. That's when the ringing in your ears
is a tumor, that's when I'm standing in the hospice,
that's when you can't live without me
but have to. That's when, oh God, even the soft night breathing
     of the
boy in the next room stops and I force myself to see his empty
     bed.

I'm sick of bringing death into our home.
The life you light in me is his lantern.
I'm doing all I can not to think of him and here he comes, pitch-
     ing his
beautiful slack tent of skin and bones right at our doorstep.

To comfort me, we lie in bed and talk of our three-year-old son.
You've taught him his full name, address and number, to say
     Brooklyn
correctly which he tries in his mouth again and again.
Mommy, he says, it's BARUCH, BARUCH-lyn, finding the He-
     brew word Baruch
meaning Blessed in the old Dutch town of Brooklyn, which you
     remind me
also means a broken land.

about the poets

Agha Shahid Ali (1949–2001) was born in New Delhi, grew up Muslim in Kashmir, and was later educated at the University of Kashmir, Srinagar, and University of Delhi. He earned a Ph.D. in English from Pennsylvania State University and an M.F.A. from the University of Arizona. His volumes of poetry include *Call Me Ishmael Tonight: A Book of Ghazals; Rooms Are Never Finished; The Country Without a Post Office;* and *Bone Sculpture.*

Karen Alkalay-Gut, born in London and raised in Rochester, New York, is a Yiddish and English poet. She is the author of *The Love of Clothes and Nakedness; In My Skin; Mechitza; Making Love; Ignorant Armies;* and others. Her poems have appeared in many publications, including *Home Planet News, Jerusalem Review, Long Shot, Tel Aviv Review,* and *PEN International.* She settled in Israel in 1972.

Nuar Alsadir received her B.A. from Amherst College, and both an M.A. in creative writing and a Ph.D. in English literature from New York University. Her poems and essays have appeared in numerous periodicals, including *Slate, Ploughshares, The Kenyon Review, Grand Street, The New York Times Magazine, AGNI, Bookforum,* and *Tin House.* She lives in Brooklyn with her husband and two daughters.

John A. Armstrong is the author of *Harvest: A Melange Relating to Brooklyn City in Particular and to the World Generally.* He worked as a counsellor at law and was a frequent contributor to the daily paper *Brooklyn.*

L.S. Asekoff is the associate professor and coordinator of the program in poetry at Brooklyn College; he received his M.A. from Brandeis. His poems have appeared in *The New Yorker, Poetry, Tikkun, Salmagundi, TriQuarterly,* and *The American Poetry Review.* He has published two volumes of poetry, *Dreams of Work* (Orchises, 1994) and *North Star* (Orchises, 1997).

Andrea Baker was born in 1976 in Madison, Wisconsin, and was raised in Jacksonville, Florida. *Like Wind Loves a Window,* her first full-length collection, was selected by Donald Revell for the 2004 Slope Editions Prize. She is also the author of the chapbook *Gilda,* which was selected by Claudia Rankine for a Poetry Society of America Fellowship. Her poems have appeared in journals such as *Denver Quarterly, Drunken Boat, Fence, How2, Lit, Octopus, Slope, St. Elizabeth Street, Vert,* and *Volt.* She lives in Brooklyn.

Amiri Baraka was born LeRoi Jones in Newark, New Jersey, in 1934. After attending Howard University in Washington, D.C., he served in the United States Air Force. He became a nationally prominent artist in 1964, with the New York production of his Obie Award–winning play *Dutchman.* After the death of Malcolm X, he became a Black Nationalist. In the mid-1970s, abandoning Cultural Nationalism, he became a Third World Marxist-Leninist. In 1999, after teaching for twenty years in the Department of Africana Studies at SUNY-Stony Brook, he retired. However, in retirement he is as active and productive as an artist and intellectual as he has ever been in his career. He lives with his wife, the poet Amina Baraka, in Newark.

Stanley Barkan was born in East New York, Brooklyn, in 1936. He has been a teacher, poet, translator, and editor of the Cross-Cultural Review Series of World Literature & Art in Sound, Print, and Motion, which has to date published 350 titles in 50 languages. He is the author of twelve poetry collections, four of which are bilingual editions. His latest book is *Mishpochech.* Barkan lives with his artist-wife, Bebe, in Merrick, New York.

Ed Barrett teaches in the MIT Writing Program. His most recent book is *Rub Out,* a trilogy of experimental verse novels.

Melissa Beattie-Moss was born in New York City in 1965. She received her B.A. in English and Women's Studies from the State University of New York at Albany and her M.F.A. from Brooklyn College. Her work has appeared in *Kalliope, Hanging Loose, California State Quarterly, Brooklyn Review,* and elsewhere. She lives with her family in State College, Pennsylvania.

Joshua Beckman was born in New Haven, Connecticut, and earned his B.A. from Hampshire College, where he studied poetry and the art of the book. His books of poetry include *Nice Hat. Thanks; Something I Expected to Be Different;* and *Things Are Happening.* He has had work published in *Harper's, Grand Street,* and *Massachusetts Review.* Beckman has taught at the Rhode Island School of Design and Hampshire College; he lives in San Francisco.

Ted Berrigan (1934–1983) completed his formal education at the University of Tulsa. He wrote more than twenty books, including *A Certain Slant of Sunlight; Many Happy Returns; Seventeen* (with Ron Padgett); *Red Wagon; In a Blue River;* and *The Sonnets.* He taught at numerous colleges and universities, including the St. Mark's Poetry Project, the Iowa Writers' Workshop, and the Naropa Institute. He is commonly called a second-generation New York School poet.

Elizabeth Bishop (1911–1979) was born in Worcester, Massachusetts, and lived for many years in Brazil. Her collections include *The Complete Poems, 1927–1979; Geography III; The Ballad of the Burglar of Babylon;* and *North and South.* She received the Pulitzer Prize and the National Book Award, among many other honors.

Juanita Brunk is the author of *Brief Landing on the Earth's Surface,* winner of the Brittingham Prize in Poetry; *Heartbreak;* and *All Sweet Things Are Falling.* Her poems have appeared in *The American Poetry Review, Passages North, Cimarron Review, Southern Poetry Review,* and *Poet Lore.* She was born in Newport News, Virginia, and now lives in New York with her husband and son.

Hayden Carruth was born in 1921. He is the author of more than thirty books of poetry, criticism, essays, a novel, and two anthologies, including *Scrambled Eggs and Whiskey, Doctor Jazz,* and *Collected Shorter Poems.* He has taught at Syracuse University and has served as editor of *Poetry,* poetry editor of *Harper's,* and as the advisory editor of *The Hudson Review.* Some of his many awards include fellowships from the Bollingen and Guggenheim Foundations, the Lenore Marshall Award, Paterson Poetry Prize, Carl Sandburg Award, Whiting Award, the Ruth Lily Prize, and the Lannon Literary Award. He lives in Munnsville, New York.

Fran Castan, a native of Brooklyn, moved to Hong Kong with her six-month-old daughter and her first husband, Sam Castan, when he became Asia bureau chief of *Look* magazine. He had reported from Vietnam for three years prior to that assignment, but was killed only six months after the couple made their home in the Far East. In the time since, Ms. Castan has worked as an editorial assistant at the *New Yorker,* an editor at Scholastic Magazines, and as the editorial director of Learning Corporation, the former educational subsidiary of Columbia Pictures. She first began to write poetry at the age of forty. Her poems have appeared in *Ms., Poetry,* and the anthology *The Seasons of Women.* Her collection of poems, *The Widow's Quilt,* was published by Canio's Editions in 1996.

Joseph L. Chester (1821–1882) is the author of *Greenwood Cemetery: and Other Poems*. He desired that his poetry be read beyond its literary value, be taken with pleasure and appreciation. His poetry was published in many newspapers and magazines and was set to music by various composers.

Amy Clampitt (1920–1994) was born in New Providence, Iowa. A graduate of Grinnell College, she lived for many years in New York City. Although she wrote poems as an adolescent, Clampitt worked at various jobs before she began to write and publish her poetry. In 1983, she published her first collection, *The Kingfisher*. Her other collections are *What the Light Was Like; Archaic Figure; Westward;* and *A Silence Opens*. Clampitt received the Fellowship of The Academy of American Poets, a MacArthur Foundation Fellowship, and a Guggenheim Fellowship.

Although he published only two books in his lifetime, Hart Crane (1899–1932) established his place in the modern literary canon with his book-length poem "The Bridge," which reflects his admiration of both Walt Whitman and his contemporary, T. S. Eliot. Crane's education was informal, at the age of seventeen he moved from Cleveland to New York. He gained fame with the publication of *The Bridge* in 1930. He was awarded a Guggenheim in 1931 and settled in Mexico to work on a long poem about the Aztec civilization. He took his own life the next year on a trip back to New York.

Enid Dame, born in 1943 in Beaver Falls, Pennsylvania, lived for many years in Brooklyn, where she edited the literary tabloid *Home Planet News* with her husband, Donald Lev. Dame was a fiction writer as well as a poet. Her collections of poetry included *Anything You Don't See, Lilith and Her Demons*, and *On the Road to Damascus, Maryland*. Enid Dame died on December 25, 2003. This anthology is dedicated to her memory.

W. E. Davenport (1862–1944) was born in New York City. He is the author of *Poetical Sermons, Visions of the City, The Perpetual Fire, The Man* (a poem in three parts representing the development of the Christian idea in history, society, and nature), *Social Settlement Sonnets,* and others.

No biographical information could be found about the writer Jean Davis, author of the poem "Our Camilla."

Mary DiLucia has published poetry as well as a number of scholarly articles in various publications, including the *American Academy in Rome Newsletter; Harvard Review,* and *Commonweal Magazine*. She has taught at Villanova University and at Harvard, where she also earned her Ph.D. and M.A.

Diane di Prima was born in Brooklyn, New York, in 1934. She co-founded the New York Poets Theatre, and founded the Poets Press, which published the work of many new writers of the Beat period. She edited a literary newsletter, *The Floating Bear,* with Amiri Baraka. Later, in northern California, she took part in the political activities of the Diggers; lived in a late-sixties commune; studied Zen Buddhism, Sanskrit, and alchemy; and raised her five children. From 1980 to 1986 she taught hermetic and esoteric traditions in poetry at the New College of California. She now lives and works in San Francisco, where she is one of the co-founders and teachers of the San Francisco Institute of Magical and Healing Arts. She is the author of thirty-five books of poetry and prose, including *Pieces of a Song, The Poetry Deal,* and *Recollections of My Life as a Woman.* Her work has been translated into at least twenty languages. She has received grants for her poetry from the National Endowment for the Arts. In 1993, she received an Award for Lifetime Achievement in Poetry from the National Poetry Association.

Brooklyn native Alan Dugan (1923–2003) published seven collections of poems in his lifetime. His *Poems Seven: New and Complete Poetry* (Seven Stories Press, 2001) received the National Book Award. His other honors include the Pulitzer Prize, the Prix de Rome, the Shelley Memorial Award from the Poetry Society of America, and the Yale Series of Younger Poets. He was associated for many years with the Fine Arts Work Center in Provincetown, Massachusetts. He and his wife, the artist Judith Shahn, made their home in Truro, Massachusetts.

Cornelius Eady was born in Rochester, New York, in 1954. He is the author of *Brutal Imagination; You Don't Miss Your Water; The Gathering of My Name,* a Pulitzer Prize nominee; *BOOM BOOM BOOM; Victims of the Latest Dance Craze,* which was the Lamont Poetry Selection of The Academy of American Poets; and *Kartunes* (1980). He is Associate Professor of English and Director of the Poetry Center at the State University of New York at Stony Brook. He lives in New York City.

Martín Espada was born in Brooklyn, New York, in 1957. Espada's books of poetry include *Alabanza: New and Selected Poems; A Mayan Astronomer in Hell's Kitchen: (1982–2002); Imagine the Angels of Bread; City of Coughing and Dead Radiators; Rebellion is the Circle of a Lover's Hands,* a bilingual collection; and *Trumpets from the Islands of Their Eviction.* He has edited several anthologies, including *El Coro: A Chorus of Latino and Latina Poets and Poetry Like Bread: Poets of the Political Imagination.* His prose collection, *Zapata's Disciple: Essays,* was published in 1998. The recipient of numerous awards and fellowships, his honors include the American Book Award, PEN/Voelker Award for

Poetry, the Paterson Poetry Prize, two fellowships from the National Endowment for the Arts, a PEN/Revson fellowship, and a Massachusetts Artists Foundation fellowship. Martín Espada lives with his wife and son in Amherst, Massachusetts, where he is an Associate Professor of English at the University of Massachusetts-Amherst.

Irving Feldman was born in Brooklyn in 1928. He was educated at the City College of New York and at Columbia University. Feldman's collections of poetry include *Beautiful False Things: Poems; All of Us Here*, a finalist for the National Book Critics Circle Award; *Leaping Clear* and *The Pripet Marshes*, both finalists for the National Book Award; and *Works and Days. The Life and Letters* was a finalist for the Poets' Prize. He lives in Buffalo, New York, and is Distinguished Professor of English at the State University of New York at Buffalo.

One of the prominent figures of the Beat Generation, Lawrence Ferlinghetti was born in Yonkers in 1919. He studied at the University of North Carolina, Columbia University, and the Sorbonne. Ferlinghetti is the author of more than thirty books of poetry, including *San Francisco Poems; How to Paint Sunlight; A Far Rockaway of the Heart; These Are My Rivers: New & Selected Poems, 1955–1993; Over All the Obscene Boundaries: European Poems & Transitions; Who Are We Now?; The Secret Meaning of Things;* and *A Coney Island of the Mind.* He has translated the work of a number of poets, including Nicanor Parra, Jacques Prevert, and Pier Paolo Pasolini. He is also the author of more than eight plays and of the novels *Love in the Days of Rage* and *Her.* One of the co-founders of City Lights Books, Ferlinghetti has served as both editor-in-chief and owner for fifty years. He lives in San Francisco, where he serves as the city's first poet laureate.

Philip Freneau (1752–1832) attended Princeton, intending to become a minister, but found his calling in literature. Political concerns led James Madison, Freneau, and their friends to revive the defunct Plain Dealing Club as the American Whig Society. Charged with literary and political enthusiasm, Freneau and Hugh Henry Brackenridge collaborated on *Father Bombo's Pilgrimage to Mecca in Arabia,* which presents comic glimpses of life in eighteenth-century America. This piece may well be the first work of prose fiction written in America. Freneau wrote two collections of poetry, *Poems Relating to the American Revolution* and *Poems from the War of 1812.*

Joanna Fuhrman was born in New York and lives in Brooklyn. Her poems have appeared in such publications as *American Poetry: Next Genera-*

tion, and *Lit,* and she has published two books through Brooklyn-based Hanging Loose Press: *Ugh Ugh Ocean* and *Freud in Brooklyn.*

Jonathan Galassi is a poet, a translator, and an executive editor at Farrar, Straus and Giroux. He is also the former Chairman of The Academy of American Poets. He is the author of the poetry collections *Morning Run* and *North Street.* His translations include the works of Eugenio Montale, including *The Second Life of Art: Selected Essays* and *Otherwise: Last and First Poems.* Galassi is the winner of the Weidenfeld Translation Prize (UK) and the Premio Montale (Italy). He lives in Brooklyn.

David Gershator lives in St. Thomas but still considers himself a Brooklyn writer. He grew up in Williamsburg, near Bushwick, and has taught at Brooklyn College, among other schools, and has lived in Downtown Brooklyn. His work has appeared in *The Caribbean Writer* and *Home Planet News,* as well as other journals, chapbooks, and anthologies.

Allen Ginsberg (1926–1997) was born in Newark, New Jersey. As a student at Columbia University in the 1940s, he began close friendships with William S. Burroughs, Neal Cassady, and Jack Kerouac, leading figures of the Beat movement. In 1954, Ginsberg moved to San Francisco. His first book of poems, *Howl,* overcame censorship trials to become one of the most widely read book of poems of the century, translated into more than twenty-two languages. He went on to co-found and direct the Jack Kerouac School of Disembodied Poetics at the Naropa Institute in Colorado. In his later years he became a Distinguished Professor at Brooklyn College. His other works include *Kaddish and Other Poems, 1958–1960; Selected Poems, 1947–1955;* and a rock CD titled *The Ballad of the Skeletons.*

Geoffrey Godbert's poetry has appeared in *Gnosis, Acumen, Nineties Poetry, Completing the Picture,* and *Earth Ascending.* He won the *Dada Dance* award for his poem "Counting Time." His collections of poetry include *I Was Not, Was Not, Mad Today: New Poems; The Ides of March; The Brooklyn Bridge; Are You Interested in Tattooing;* and others. Godbert has also worked as co-editor with Harold Pinter and Anthony Astbury on *100 Poems by 100 Poets* and *99 Poems in Translation.* He is co-founder of the Greville Press and established the poetry magazines *The Third Eye* and *Only Poetry.* He lives in Somerset, England.

Jessica Greenbaum was born in Brooklyn and grew up on Long Island. She earned a B.A. from Barnard College and was a member of the first graduating class of the University of Houston's Creative Writing Program. Her first collection of poems, *Inventing Difficulty,* won the 1998 Gerard Cable Book Award. She has also received a "Discovery"/*The Na-*

tion prize and PEN's New Writer award. Her poems, criticism, and personal essays have appeared in *Boulevard, The Nation, The New Yorker, The Village Voice,* and the *Women's Review of Books,* among other publications. She has taught at Barnard College and Pratt Institute and lives in Brooklyn.

Marilyn Hacker was born in New York City in 1942. She attended the Washington Square College of New York University and the Arts Students League. Hacker was editor of *The Kenyon Review* from 1990 to 1994. She is the author of several books of poetry, including *Desperanto: Poems, 1999–2002; Squares and Courtyards; Winter Numbers; Selected Poems, 1965–1990; Love, Death, and the Changing of the Seasons; Assumptions; Taking Notice; Going Back to the River; Separations;* and *Presentation Piece.* She lives in New York City and Paris.

Kimiko Hahn is the author of *Air Pocket, Earshot,* which was awarded the Theodore Roethke Memorial Poetry Prize and an Association of Asian American Studies Literature Award; *The Unbearable Heart,* which received an American Book Award; *Volatile; The Artist's Daughter;* and *Mosquito and Ant.* In 1995 she wrote ten portraits of women for a two-hour HBO special entitled "Ain't Nuthin But a She-thing." She is a recipient of fellowships from the National Endowment for the Arts, and the New York Foundation for the Arts, as well as a Lila Wallace/Reader's Digest Writers' Award. Kimiko Hahn is an Associate Professor in the English Department at Queens College/CUNY.

Daniel Hall was born in 1952. His third collection, *Under Sleep,* will be published by the University of Chicago Press in 2007. His other collections include *Hermit with Landscape,* which was chosen for the Yale Series of Younger Poets, and *Strange Relation,* selected by Mark Doty for the National Poetry Series. He has been the winner of the "Discovery"/*The Nation* award, and grants from the Ingram Merrill Foundation and the National Endowment for the Arts. He also traveled through Asia as an Amy Lowell Traveling Scholar. He lives in Amherst, Massachusetts.

Joelle Hann has lived on Grand Street, in Williamsburg, Brooklyn, since 1998. She has published poems in such journals as *The Brooklyn Rail, Mc-Sweeney's, La Petite Zine,* and *Painted Bride Quarterly,* and from 2001 to 2004 she curated the Waxpoetic Reading Series at Pete's Candy Store. She works as an editor for Bedford/St. Martin's and is currently learning Portuguese.

Michael S. Harper was born in Brooklyn, New York, in 1938. He earned a B.A. and M.A. from what is now known as California State University, and an M.F.A. from the University of Iowa. He has published more than ten books of poetry, including *Songlines in Michaeltree: New and Collected*

Poems; Honorable Amendments; Healing Song for the Inner Ear; Images of Kin, which won the Melville-Cane Award from the Poetry Society of America and was nominated for the National Book Award; *Nightmare Begins Responsibility; History Is Your Heartbeat,* which won the Black Academy of Arts & Letters Award for poetry; and *Dear John, Dear Coltrane.* He was the first Poet Laureate of the State of Rhode Island (1988–1993). Michael S. Harper is University Professor and Professor of English at Brown University, where he has taught since 1970.

Jeffrey Harrison is the author of *Singing Underneath,* published by the National Poetry Series, *Signs of Arrival,* and *Feeding the Fire.* His poems have also appeared in *Poetry, The New Yorker, The Nation, The Paris Review, Partisan Review, The New Republic,* and others. He attended Columbia University, Stanford University, and the University of Iowa. Some of his honors include the Peter I. B. Lavan Award from the Academy of American Poets, the Amy Lowell Travelling Poetry Scholarship, and fellowships from the Ingram Merrill Foundation and the National Endowment for the Arts. He lives in Connecticut with his family.

Steven Hartman was born in Storm Lake, Iowa, and has lived in Brooklyn since he arrived via the U.S. Navy in 1968. He received a B.A. and an M.B.A. from Long Island University's Brooklyn Center. He has published poems in *Home Planet News, The Ledge,* and *Metrosphere,* and performed his work at ABC No Rio, the Back Fence, and the Lismar Lounge. He is founder of Pinched Nerves Press, and author of several chapbooks, including *Swimming with Sharks, Ding Dong Dada,* and *Pinched Nerves,* and has edited the little magazine *Make Room for Dada.*

Robert Hershon has worked as co-editor at Hanging Loose Press and been a contributor since the first issue of the Press's magazine. His poems have appeared in such publications as *Poetry Northwest, Poetry East, Telephone,* and *The Nation,* as well as anthologies and ten collections of his own, including *How to Ride on the Woodlawn Express, SUN,* and *The Public Hug; New and Selected Poems.* He has won writing fellowships from the National Endowment for the Arts and the Creative Artists Public Service Program. He lives in Brooklyn.

David Ignatow (1914–1997) was born in Brooklyn, and lived most of his life in New York. He published sixteen volumes of poetry and three prose collections. Included in these are *Poems, The Gentle Weightlifter, Say Pardon, Figures of the Human, Earth Hard: Selected Poems, Rescue the Dead, Facing the Tree, Tread the Dark, Whisper to the Earth, Leaving the Door Open, Shadowing the Ground, Against the Evidence,* and *I Have a Name.* His work was recognized with the Bollingen Prize, two Guggenheim fellowships, the Wallace Stevens fellowship from Yale University, the Rockefeller Foundation fellowship, the Poetry Society of America's Shelly Memorial Award, and an award from the National Endowment for the Arts. He was president emeritus of the Poetry Society of America and a member of the executive board of the Walt Whitman Birthplace Association.

Gale Jackson is a poet, writer, storyteller, librarian, and an organizer in cultural education. Her work has been published in *Callaloo, Freedomways, IKON, Essence Magazine, The Women's Quarterly Journal,* and others. She is a co-editor for *Art Against Apartheid,* a reviewer of children's books, and a lecturer. She lives in Brooklyn, where she works as a librarian and instructor at Medgar Evers College of the City University of New York.

Lisa Jarnot was born in Buffalo, New York, in 1967. She attended State University of New York at Buffalo and Brown University. She has been the editor of two small poetry magazines, *No Trees* and *Troubled Surfer,* and was also editor of *The St Mark's Poetry Project Newsletter* until 1997. Jarnot is currently teaching at the Naropa Institute's Jack Kerouac School for Disembodied Poetics. She is the author of *Ring of Fire, Sea Lyrics, Some Other Kind of Mission, The Eightfold Path,* and other books, and the co-editor of *An Anthology of New American Poets.* She starred in the 2004 film *The Time We Killed,* directed by Jennifer Todd Reeves. Jarnot lives and writes in New York.

Hettie Jones was born Hettie Cohen in Brooklyn, New York, in 1934. She earned a B.A. in Drama from the University of Virginia and did postgraduate work at Columbia University. Her works include *Drive; How I Became Hettie Jones,* a memoir of the beat scene of the fifties and sixties, as well as of her marriage to Amiri Baraka; *Big Star Fallin' Mama: Five Women in Black Music;* and several books for children. Her fiction, poems, and prose have appeared in *Essence, Frontier: A Journal of Women Studies, Hanging Loose, Heresies, IKON, Ploughshares, Village, Washington Post,* and others. She established *Yugen* with Amiri Baraka, a magazine that published poetry and writings by William Burroughs, Allen Ginsberg, Philip Whalen, and Jack Kerouac. She also launched Totem Press, which published poets such as Ginsberg, Gregory Corso, and Frank O'Hara. She is currently involved with PEN American Center's Prison Writing committee and runs a writing workshop at the New York State Correctional Facility for Women at Bedford Hills. Hettie Jones lives in New York City.

Patricia Spears Jones, born in Arkansas in 1955, is a widely published poet, arts writer, and playwright. Her works include *The Weather That*

Kills, and *Mother,* produced by Mabou Mines in 1994. Her poems and other writings have appeared in *The Poetry Project Newsletter, Ploughshares, Village Voice, Essence, Boston Globe,* and *Heliotrope,* and online in *bkyn: an online journal of the arts,* and have been widely anthologized. She also writes on the visual and performing arts and is the co-editor of *Ordinary Women: An Anthology of New York City Women* (1978). Formerly a teacher at Sarah Lawrence, Jones currently teaches creative writing at Parsons and the 14th Street Y in New York. She lives in New York City.

June Jordan (1936–2002) was born in New York City. Her books of poetry include *Kissing God Goodbye: Poems, 1991–1997, Haruko/Love Poems, Naming Our Destiny: New and Selected Poems, Living Room, Passion,* and *Things That I Do in the Dark.* She is also the author of children's books, plays, a novel, and *Poetry for the People: A Blueprint for the Revolution,* a guide to writing, teaching, and publishing poetry. Her collections of political essays include *Affirmative Acts: Political Essays* and *Technical Difficulties.* Basic Books published her memoir, *Soldier: A Poet's Childhood,* in 2000. She taught at the University of California, Berkeley, where she founded Poetry for the People.

Born in Lithuania, Menke Katz (1906–1991) emigrated at the age of nine. A kabbalist, teacher of Yiddish and folklore, and poetic innovator, he published nine books of poetry in Yiddish and nine in English. His work was published in *Poetry, Atlantic,* and *New York Times,* and for thirty years he edited the poetry magazine *Bitterroot.*

Diane Kendig was born in Canton, Ohio. She attended Otterbein College and received an M.A. in English from Cleveland State University. She has taught high school Spanish and English, English at CSU and at Cuyahoga Community College. Kendig is a participating poet in the Ohio Arts Council's Artist-in-Residence program. Her works include *A Tunnel of Flute Song* and *Greatest Hits: 1978–2000.* She is also the translator of *And a Pencil to Write Your Name: Poems from the Nicaraguan Poetry Workshop.*

Maurice Kenny, Mohawk, was born in Watertown, New York, in 1929. He was educated at Butler University, St. Lawrence University, and New York University. He has been the co-editor of the literary review magazine *Contact/II* as well as the editor/publisher of Strawberry Press. He has also been poetry editor of *Adirondack Magazine.* Maurice's work has been published in almost one hundred journals, including *Trends, American Indian Quarterly, Blue Cloud Quarterly, Saturday Review, New York Times, Calaloo,* and *World Literature Today.* He has been director of The Little Gallery and is currently art director of the Blue Moon Cafe, both in Saranac Lake. His collections include *North: Poems of Home; Only As Far As*

Brooklyn, combining his gay and Indian consciousness; *The Mama Poems; Blackrobe;* and *Dancing Back Strong the Nation.*

Galway Kinnell was born in Providence, Rhode Island, in 1927. He studied at Princeton University and the University of Rochester. His volumes of poetry include *A New Selected Poems,* a finalist for the National Book Award; *Imperfect Thirst; When One Has Lived a Long Time Alone; Selected Poems,* for which he received both the Pulitzer Prize and the National Book Award; *Mortal Acts, Mortal Words; The Book of Nightmares; Body Rags; Flower Herding on Mount Monadnock;* and *What a Kingdom It Was.* He has also published translations of works by Yves Bonnefroy, Yvanne Goll, and François Villon, and Rainer Maria Rilke. He was the Erich Maria Remarque Professor of Creative Writing at New York University for many years, and a Chancellor of The Academy of American Poets. Kinnell retired from teaching in 2005.

Noelle Kocot was born, raised, and now lives in Brooklyn. She earned her B.A. from Oberlin College and her M.F.A. from the University of Florida. She has been awarded a fellowship from the National Endowment for the Arts. Her poetry collections are *Poem for the End of Time and Other Poems* (Wave Books, 2006), *The Raving Fortune* (2004), and *4* (2001). Her poems have appeared in *The American Poetry Review, Anodyne, Fence, Conduit, Lilliput Review, LIT, New American Writing,* and others.

Anthony Lacavaro has lived in Brooklyn since 1998. He is a contributing editor to *Open City* magazine and books.

Joan Larkin lives and writes in Brooklyn. She has taught on the faculties of Brooklyn, Goddard, and Sarah Lawrence colleges. Her collections of poetry include *Housework, A Long Sound,* and *Cold River.* Other works include *The Living,* a play; *Sor Juana's Love Poems,* a translation; and *Glad Day,* a book of meditation for lesbian, gay, and bisexual, and transgender people. She is co-editor of *Living Out,* a gay and lesbian autobiography series published by the University of Wisconsin Press. She has received fellowships in poetry and playwriting from the National Endowment for the Arts, and the Massachusetts Cultural Council.

Katherine Lederer was educated at the University of California, Berkeley, and the University of Iowa. She is the author of the memoir *Poker Face: A Girlhood Among Gamblers* and the poetry collection *Winter Sex.* She lives in New York City.

Rika Lesser is a poet and translator of Swedish and German literature. She has published three collections of original poetry, including *Growing*

Back: Poems 1972–1992, and has translated the poetry of Claes Andersson, Gunnar Ekelöf, Rainer Maria Rilke, and Göran Sonnevi. Her translation of Sonnevi's selected poems, *A Child Is Not a Knife* (1993), won several awards, and in 1996 she was awarded the Poetry Translation Prize of the Swedish Academy. Her translation of *Guide to the Underworld*, by Gunnar Ekelöf, was awarded the Landon Poetry Translation Prize from the Academy of American Poets. Born in Brooklyn, Rika Lesser has taught literary translation at Columbia and Yale.

Donald Lev was born in 1936. He attended Hunter College, worked the wire rooms of the *Daily News* and *The New York Times,* and drove a taxi for twenty years. He has contributed poetry to *The Village Voice* and *HYN Anthology* (his own small-press magazine). He has published many collections of poetry, including *Intercourse with the Dead, Peculiar Merriment, Footnotes, Enemies of Time,* and *Twilight.* He was married to the late poet Enid Dame, with whom he co-edited the literary tabloid *Home Planet News* and lived at Brighton Beach. He now lives in upstate New York.

Phillis Levin is the author of the poetry collections *Mercury, The Afterimage* and *Temples and Fields.* She edited *The Penguin Book of the Sonnet: 500 Years of a Classic Tradition in English.*

Philip Levine was born in Detroit, Michigan, in 1928, and educated in local schools and at Wayne State University. He has published collections at regular intervals since *On the Edge* appeared in 1963, some of these include *Not This Pig, Animals Are Passing from Our Lives, They Feed The Lion, The Horse, 1933,* and *Francisco, I'll Bring You Red Carnations.* Levine has periodically lived in Spain, a country whose people, landscape, and history remain a strong presence in his poems. He is now Professor of English at California State University in Fresno.

Mani Leyb (Brahinski) (1883–1953) was a Yiddish poet from Niezhin, Chernigov, Ukraine. He immigrated to the New York in 1905. A skilled bootmaker, he worked in shoe factories until he was forced to quit after contracting tuberculosis. He was the leading figure of *Di Yunge.* He translated widely from Russian and Ukrainian as part of an arrangement with the *Jewish Daily Forward (Forverts),* which published poets weekly, originals or translations.

Matthew Lippman is the author of the poetry collection *The New Year of Yellow,* and his poetry has appeared in such journals as *The American Poetry Review, The Iowa Review, The Best American Poetry of 1997,* and *Spinning Jenny.* He has taught at the University of Iowa, Westchester Community College,

Columbia University, and Roslyn High School. He holds a B.A. from Hobart College, an M.F.A. in poetry from the University of Iowa, and an M.A. in English education from Columbia University.

Timothy Liu (Liu Ti Mo) was born in San Jose, California, in 1965, to parents from China. He is the author of *For Dust Thou Art; Of Thee I Sing; Hard Evidence; Say Goodnight,* which was a finalist for the Lambda Literary Award; *Burnt Offerings;* and *Vox Angelica,* which won the Poetry Society of America's Norma Farber First Book Award. He has also edited *Word of Mouth: An Anthology of Gay American Poetry.* His poems have been included in more than twenty anthologies and have appeared in such magazines and journals as *Antioch Review, Grand Street, Chelsea, Kenyon Review, Paris Review, Ploughshares, Poetry,* and *TriQuarterly.* He lives in Hoboken, New Jersey.

Audre Lorde (1934–1992) was born in New York City as Audrey Geraldine Lorde. She was the daughter of Caribbean immigrants who settled in Harlem. She graduated from Columbia University and Hunter College, where she later held the prestigious post of Thomas Hunter Chair of Literature. She received many awards and honors, including the Walt Whitman Citation of Merit, a National Endowment for the Arts grant, and the New York State's Poet Laureate. Her first poem was published in *Seventeen* magazine while she was still in high school. Lorde went on to publish more than a dozen books of poetry, and six books of prose. Lorde worked as a librarian, and as a teacher at Tougaloo College. She co-founded the Kitchen Table: Women of Color Press, and was the founder of the Sisterhood in Support of Sisters in South Africa. Her works include *The First Cities, Cables to Rage, From a Land Where Other People Live, Coal,* and *The Black Unicorn.*

Federico García Lorca (1898–1936) was born in Fuente Vaqueros, Granada, Spain. He was one of the great Spanish writers and artists of the twentieth century. In his short lifetime he produced a wide variety of novels, short stories, poetry, as well as paintings, drawings, and even musical compositions. He influenced such politically disparate artists as the poet Neruda and the painter Salvador Dali. In 1929, García Lorca came to New York, returning to Spain in 1930 after the proclamation of the Spanish Republic. Much of his work was infused with popular themes such as flamenco and Gypsy culture. Some of his poetic works include *Lament for the Death of a Bullfighter and Other Poems* and *Impresiones y Viajes Libro de poemas,* a compilation of poems based on Spanish folklore. *Romancero Gitano* (The Gypsy ballads) brought García Lorca far-reaching fame; it was reprinted seven times during his lifetime. He was also the author of plays, including *El Maleficio de la mariposa, Bodas de sangre, Yerma, La Casa de Bernarda*

Alba, and others. On August 19, 1936, at the age of thirty-eight, Lorca was beaten to death by Franco's Falangists, along with several other political opponents of Franco. His books were burned in Granada's Plaza del Carmen and were soon banned from Franco's Spain.

Robert Lowell (1917–1977) was the author of several collections of poetry including *History; Lord Weary's Castle* (which won the Pulitzer Prize in 1946); *Life Studies* (winner of the National Book Award 1959); *The Dolphin* (Pulitzer Prize, 1973); and *Day by Day* (National Book Critics Circle Award 1977). He studied at Kenyon College and Louisiana State University. During WWII he refused to serve in the military and spent five months in a New York City detention center. After his death his *Collected Poems*, edited by Frank Bidart and David Gewanter, was published in 2003.

Marjorie Maddox is a professor of literature and writing at Lock Haven University. At Cornell University she gained her M.F.A. in poetry with the help of a Sage Graduate Fellowship. Her poems have been published in many literary journals and several books, including *Perpendicular as I Am*, winner of the 1994 Sandstone Poetry Award; *Nightrider to Edinburgh*, which in 1986 received the Charles William Duke Long Poem Award; *How to Fit God into a Poem* (winner of the Chapbook Award in 1993); *Ecclesia*; and *Body Parts*. She lives with her husband and children in Williamsport, Pennsylvania.

David Margolis loved Brooklyn and loved being from Brooklyn. After he moved to Jerusalem he referred to Brooklyn as "the other Ir Ha'Kodesh (Holy City)." He was the author of two novels, *Change of Partners* and *The Stepman;* a volume of short fiction, *The Time of Wandering;* and he was co-author of *The Muselmann,* a Holocaust memoir. He was the Jewish World Editor to the *Jerusalem Report* magazine, and his journalism was widely published in the United States and Israel. He died in 2005.

Charles Martin is the author of *Steal the Bacon* and *What the Darkness Proposes*, both nominated for the Pulitzer Prize; *Room for Error;* and *Starting from Sleep: New and Selected Poems*. He has also done translations of the Latin poet Catullus and of Ovid's *Metamorphoses*. His poems have appeared in *Poetry, The New Yorker, The Hudson Review, Boulevard, The Threepenny Review,* and in many other magazines and anthologies. He is a professor at Queensborough Community College (CUNY) and has taught workshops at the Sewanee Writers Conference, the West Chester Conference on Form and Narrative in Poetry, and the Unterberg Center of the 92nd Street YMCA.

Donna Masini is a professor in the M.F.A. program at Hunter College and teaches writing workshops at Columbia University. She is a recipient of a National Endowment for the Arts grant and a New York Foundation for the Arts grant. Her most recent book is the poetry collection *Turning to Fiction*. Her other works include *That Kind of Danger*, which won the Barnard Women Poets' Prize in 1994, and *About Yvonne*, a novel. Masini's poems have appeared in *Triquarterly*, *Paris Review*, *Georgia Review*, *Parnassus*, and *Boulevard*. She lives in New York City.

Vladimir Vladimirovich Mayakovsky (1893–1930), Russian poet and dramatist, was born in Bagdadi, Kutais region, Georgia. In 1906 he moved to Moscow. He was a leader of the Futurist school in 1912 and was chief poet of the Bolshevik Revolution. After the Revolution he devoted almost all his energies to propaganda verse. His plays include *Mystery Bouffe*; *The Bedbug*; *Vladimir Mayakovsky, a Tragedy*; and *The Bathhouse*. The collection of poetry and prose published in 1912 under the title *A Slap in the Face of Public Taste* contained Mayakovsky's first two published poems, entitled "Night" and "Morning." The title of the collection was also that of the famous futurist manifesto, signed by Mayakovsky, Burlyuk, Kruchonykh, and Khlebnikov. Mayakovsky also published his own books of poetry, including *Me*, *The Backbone Flute*, *War and the World*, and *Man*, which was regarded as the high point of Mayakovsky's pre-Revolutionary poetry. In 1930, Mayakovsky, disillusioned with Soviet life, committed suicide.

Marianne Moore (1887–1972) was born in St. Louis, Missouri, and educated at Bryn Mawr College. For many years she made her home in the Clinton Hill section of Brooklyn, where she lived with her mother and served for a time as editor for the literary magazine *The Dial* and as an assistant at the New York Public Library. The recipient of nearly every literary honor available to American poets, including the Pulitzer Prize and National Book Award, Moore published her *Complete Poems* in 1967. The volume attests to her enduring achievement as a poet of both exacting restraint and minutely observed images drawn from, among other favorite subjects, athletes such as the Brooklyn Dodgers and animals of all sorts.

Michael Morse teaches at the Ethical Culture Fieldston School, Gotham Writers' Workshop, and the Iowa Summer Writing Festival. Publishing credits include *A Public Space*, *The Literary Review*, *Ploughshares*, and *Tin House*. He was nominated for Pushcart Prizes in 2002 and 2005. After stints in the Brooklyn neighborhoods of Cobble Hill, Boreum Hill, and Carroll Gardens, he currently resides in Red Hook.

Howard Moss (1922–1987) was born and raised in New York City. In 1942, he won *Poetry* magazine's Janet Sewall David Award for his poetry. He was inducted into the American Academy and Institute of Arts and Letters in 1968, and won the National Book Award for poetry for his *Selected Poems* in 1971. His *New Selected Poems* was awarded the Lenore Marshall / *Nation* Poetry Prize in 1986; in that year he also received a fellowship from the Academy of American Poets. He also worked as poetry editor of *The New Yorker.*

Maggie Nelson is from northern California. Her work has appeared in *The Best American Poetry 2002, Heights of the Marvelous: A New York Anthology, the Hat, LIT,* and *Shiny.* She is the founding editor of the literary magazine *Fort Necessity* and has taught at Wesleyan University and the New School Graduate Writing Program in creative writing. She lives in Brooklyn.

D. Nurkse, a former poet laureate of Brooklyn, is the author of eight poetry collections, including *Burnt Island* and *The Fall.* His other accolades include the Bess Hokin Prize from *Poetry* magazine, two grants from the National Endowment for the Arts, a Tanne Foundation Award, and the Whiting Writers' Award. For many years he has lived in Brooklyn's Windsor Terrace.

Ed Ochester was born in 1939 in Brooklyn and educated at Cornell University, Harvard University, and the University of Wisconsin. His poems have appeared in *American Poetry Review, The North American Review, Ploughshares,* and many others. His books of poetry include *Changing the Name to Ochester, Miracle Mile,* and *Dancing on the Edges of Knives,* which won the Devins Award for Poetry. He has served as the general editor of the Pitt Poetry Series and is founding editor of the poetry magazine *5 A.M.* He is the author of *Unreconstructed New and Selected Poems,* and he teaches at the Bennington MFA Writing Seminars.

One of the leading poets of the New York School, Frank O'Hara (1926–1966) was also the curator of the international program at the Museum of Modern Art and an editorial associate for *Art News.* Prior to his untimely death in a car accident on Fire Island, O'Hara worked on a number of collaborations with visual artists, as well as on his own poetry. His *Collected Poems,* published posthumously in 1971, won the National Book Award.

Perhaps the most notable of the Objectivists, George Oppen (1908–1984) was born in New Rochelle, New York. Founding the Objectivist Press in the 1920s, Oppen published his first book *Discrete Series* in 1934. After he and his wife, Mary, joined the Communist Party in

1935, Oppen went on to serve in the Second World War, and was gravely injured. Targeted by the House Committee on Un-American Activities and by Senator Joseph McCarthy, the Oppens fled to Mexico. For nearly twenty years Oppen produced no poetry, but then published many highly acclaimed subsequent volumes in the mid- and late sixties. One of these, *Of Being Numerous,* received the 1968 Pulitzer Prize. He lived in San Francisco from that time until his death.

Gabriel Preil (1911–1993) was born in Estonia and immigrated to New York in 1922. Although he also wrote in Yiddish and English, he was primarily a modern Hebrew poet. Preil's poetry appeared widely in translation in English-language magazines and in numerous anthologies, along with translations in Greek, Estonian, Hungarian, Italian, and Russian. His works include *Landscape of Sun and Frost, Candles Against the Stars, Fire and Silence, Poems from End to End,* and *Courteous to Myself,* among others. He translated many American poets, including Robert Frost and Carl Sandburg. The recipient of several literary prizes, including the New York University Newman Award and the Bialik Prize, he was also awarded an honorary degree in Hebrew Literature from the Hebrew Union College.

Alicia Jo Rabins was born in 1977. She is a poet and wandering fiddler based in Park Slope, Brooklyn. Her poetry mentors have included Kenneth Koch at Columbia and Claudia Rankine at Barnard College. She was the recipient of the 1995 Artscape Award for Poetry for her chapbook, *The Girl Who Wants to Be a Landscape* (Artscape Press); other poems have appeared in the *Boston Review* and *6 x 6* (Ugly Duckling Presse).

Charles Reznikoff (1894–1976) was born in Brooklyn to Russian immigrants who had fled political persecution following the assassination of Alexander II. One of the foremost figures of the Objectivist school, Reznikoff was a lifelong resident of New York City. His life's work is collected in *Complete Poems, 1918–1975.*

Matthew Rohrer is a poetry editor for the literary magazine *Fence.* Born in 1970 in Ann Arbor, Michigan, he lives in Brooklyn with his wife and son, and teaches at New School University. His collections of poems are *A Green Light, Satellite,* and *A Hummock in the Malookas,* winner of the National Poetry Series open competition. Rohrer earned a B.A. from the University of Michigan, where he won a Hopwood Award for poetry, and received his M.F.A. in Poetry from the University of Iowa.

Quentin Rowan was born in Brooklyn, New York, in 1976. "Prometheus at Coney Island," written in 1992 when he was sixteen years old, appeared in the Brooklyn poetry journal *Hanging Loose,* and was later chosen for inclusion in the *Best American Poetry, 1996,* edited by Adrienne Rich. At twenty, Rowan turned to writing fiction and had his first short story published in *The Paris Review* while still in college. His stories have appeared in several other magazines since, including *Bomb* and *Witness.* He is currently at work on a graphic novel, *Curious Clover.*

William Hobart Royce (1878–1963) is the author of *1940, Sonnets of a Bibliographer, Printer's Ink,* and a number of broadsides, many related to World War II. He also compiled *A Balzac Bibliography,* writings relevant to the life and works of Honoré de Balzac, and the *Bibliography of the Writings and Speeches of Gabriel Wells, L.H.D.,* along with Charles F. Heartman.

Muriel Rukeyser (1913–1980) was born in New York City. She attended the Fieldston Schools, Vassar University, and Columbia University. Rukeyser's first book of poems, *Theory of Flight,* was chosen by Stephen Vincent Benet for publication in the Yale Younger Poets Series in 1935. Rukeyser was heavily involved in political activism on a set of issues ranging from the Scottsboro case to the Spanish Civil War to feminism and the American aggression in Vietnam. She wrote for the *Daily Worker,* served as President of PEN's American Center, and traveled to Spain to cover the People's Olympiad. Her various works of poetry include *The Book of the Dead, A Turning Wind, Beast in View, The Green Wave, Elegies, Body of Waking, The Speed of Darkness, Breaking Open,* and *The Gates.* She also published biographies of Willard Gibbs, Wendell Wilkie, and Thomas Hariot; fiction; plays and screenplays; translations of work by Octavio Paz and Gunnar Ekelöff; and, in 1949, *The Life of Poetry.*

Georgine Sanders was born in 1921 in Padang, Indonesia. She studied medicine in Utrecht, the Netherlands, and there met Leo Vroman in 1938. World War II kept them apart until 1947, when they married in the United States. She was not able to finish her medical studies, but she obtained a Ph.D. in medical anthropology in 1980 in New York. A longtime resident of Brooklyn, she is the mother of two daughters and now lives in Forth Worth, Texas. Sanders has published two books of poetry in Dutch and one, collaboratively, with Mr. Vroman.

Sapphire, born Ramona Lofton in 1950, is a performance poet and author. She spent her first twelve years on army bases in California and Texas. As a teenager, she lived in South Philadelphia and Los Angeles. She graduated from City College in Harlem with a degree in dance and received an M.F.A. from Brooklyn College. Living in Harlem, she taught reading and writing to teenagers and adults. Her collections of prose and poetry include *American Dreams* and *Black Wings & Blind Angels: Poems.* She is also the author of the novel *Push.* She was the 1994 recipient of the MacArthur Foundation Scholarship in Poetry and was the first-place winner in *Downtown Magazine*'s Year of the Poet III Award for 1994. Sapphire lives in Brooklyn.

David Schubert (1913–1946) was born in New York City and spent his childhood in Detroit. He attended Amherst College and City College of New York, and later did graduate work at Columbia University. He was homeless at the age of fifteen and supported himself with various jobs including busboy, waiter, farmhand, and newsboy. Schubert lived in Brooklyn, where he was assistant editor at the Brooklyn Institute of Arts and Science. His poems have been seen in *Poetry, Forum, Smoke, The Partisan Review, The Nation,* and *This Generation.* His only book, *Initial A,* was published posthumously.

Delmore Schwartz (1913–1966) was born in Brooklyn to Romanian immigrants. He received a bachelor's degree in philosophy from New York University. He worked toward but never attained an advanced degree from Harvard, where he was hired as a Briggs-Copeland Lecturer and as an Assistant Professor. He was the youngest winner of the Bollingen Prize in poetry in 1960. He wrote and published critical essays, poetry, essays, fiction, translation, and even a children's book, including *In Dreams Begins Responsibility and Other Stories, Vaudeville for a Princess and Other Poems, Last and Lost Poems of Delmore Schwartz,* and *The Ego Is Always at the Wheel: Bagatelles.*

Hugh Seidman was born in Brooklyn in 1940 and educated at Columbia University. He is the author of *Blood Lord, Throne/Falcon/Eye,* and *People Live, They Have Lives.* His first book, *Collecting Evidence,* won the Yale Series of Younger Poets competition. He is the winner of several other awards, including two New York State poetry grants and three National Endowment for the Arts fellowships. He has taught writing at the University of Wisconsin, Yale University, Columbia University, the College of William and Mary, and other institutions. He lives in New York City, where he teaches a poetry workshop at the New School.

Henricus Selyns (1636–1701), clergyman, was born in Amsterdam, Holland. He was educated for the ministry at the University of Leyden and in 1660 was sent to America by the classis of Amsterdam to become pastor of the Reformed Dutch church of Breukelen (Brooklyn). He was also permitted to officiate on Sunday afternoons at Governor Peter Stuyvesant's farm, Bouwerie (now Bowery), New York, where he taught the unfortunate. He went back to Holland in 1664 but returned to New York City in 1682 to accept a call from the 1st Reformed Dutch Church, of which he was pastor until his death. He and his consistory obtained, in May, 1696, the first church charter issued in the colony. Few of his many original works have survived. He collected and transcribed all the records of the New York Reformed Dutch Church to the date of his own ministry. His only publications are *Poems,* translated from the Dutch into English by Henry C. Murphy, and printed in his *Anthology of the New Netherlands* in the collections of New-York Historical Society, and a Latin poem prefixed to some editions of Cotton Mather's *l'Viagnalia.*

Vijay Seshadri was born in Bangalore, India, in 1954, and grew up in Columbus, Ohio. He attended Oberlin College and received an M.F.A. from Columbia University. His collections of poems include *The Long Meadow,* winner of the James Laughlin Award, and *Wild Kingdom.* He currently teaches poetry and nonfiction writing at Sarah Lawrence College, and lives in Brooklyn with his wife and son.

Harvey Shapiro was born in Chicago. He received his B.A. from Yale University and his M.A. from Columbia University. In WWII he was a gunner in a B-17, for which service he received the Distinguished Flying Cross and the three-leafed oak Air Medal. He has taught English at Cornell University and poetry workshops at Columbia and Yale. He has worked on magazines and newspapers: *Commentary, The New Yorker, The New York Times Book Review,* and *The New York Times Magazine.* He has also worked on the editorial boards of *Poetry New York* and *Epoch.* His volumes of poetry include *National Cold Storage Company, The Eye, The Light Holds, This World,* and others. Shapiro has received a Rockefeller Foundation grant in poetry. He lives in Brooklyn.

Shulamit (Elson) is the author of *Kabbalah of Prayer—Sacred Sounds and the Soul's Journey* and *Brooklyn Bodhisattvas, A Book of Visions and Kabbalistic Poetry.* Born in Brooklyn, she now resides in upstate New York, where she is the Director of SoulSongs, The Center for Sound Healing. She is a graduate of New York University and has an M.A. in History.

John Skoyles is the author of three books of poems, all published by Carnegie-Mellon University Press: *A Little Faith, Permanent Change,* and *Definition of the Soul.* He is also the author of two prose works: *Generous Strangers,* a book of personal essays, and *Secret Frequencies: A New York Education,* a memoir. His work has appeared in *The Atlantic, Poetry, Yale Review, TriQuarterly,* and others. Born in Flushing, Queens, Skoyles recalls that when someone died, the old Italians of his neighborhood said, "Bye, bye,

Brook-a-lin," meaning the deceased had disappeared to Green-Wood Cemetery.

Tom Sleigh is the author of five collections of poetry: *After One, Waking, The Chain, The Dreamhouse,* and *The Far Side of the Earth.* His new translation of Euripedes' *Herakles* was recently published by Oxford University Press. He has received grants from the National Endowment for the Arts, the Guggenheim Foundation, and the Lila Wallace / Reader's Digest Fund, and numerous awards, including the Poetry Society of America's Shelley Award. He teaches at Hunter College.

Sara Teasdale (1884–1933), a native of St. Louis, Missouri, published several well-received collections in her lifetime: *Sonnets to Duse, and Other Poems* (1907); *Helen of Troy, and Other Poems* (1911); *Rivers to the Sea* (1915); *Love Songs* (1917), which won what is today called the Pulitzer Prize; *Flame and Shadow* (1920); *Dark of the Moon* (1926); and *Stars To-Night* (1930).

Daniel Tobin is the author of the poetry collections *Where the World Is Made, Double Life,* and *The Narrows.* He has also published the volume of criticism *Passage to the Center: Imagination and the Sacred in the Poetry of Seamus Heaney,* and numerous essays on poetry. He is Chair of the Department of Writing, Literature, and Publishing at Emerson College in Boston.

Goran Tomcic is a poet, a curator, and an artist who was born in Split, Croatia, in 1964. In 1991 his chapbook *Fragile* was published in Zagreb, Croatia. Ever since 1992, a year after emigrating to the United States, he has written his poems in English. Poems from his unpublished manuscript, *Voices from the Sea,* have appeared in many magazines, including *A Gathering of the Tribes, Prairie Schooner,* and *The Seneca Review.*

Tony Towle was born in 1939 in Manhattan, where he has lived for the greater part of his life. Some of his collections of poetry include *North, Lines for the New Year, After Dinner We Take a Drive into the Night, Works on Paper,* and *The History of Invention.* He has conducted poetry workshops with the Poetry Project of the St. Mark's Church.

Leo Vroman was born in 1915 in Gouda, the Netherlands. In 1938 he became engaged to Georgine Sanders. He escaped the German occupation of the Netherlands in 1940, but from 1942 until 1945 he was interned as a prisoner of war in Indonesia and Japan. In 1945, he moved to the United States and married Georgine in 1947. A biologist best known for discovering the process of sequential protein absorption called "the Vroman effect," he is the author of fifty books, mostly poetry. A longtime resident of Brooklyn and father of two daughters, he now lives in Forth Worth, Texas.

John Wakeman was born in London and worked as a librarian in London libraries and the Brooklyn Public Library. Back in England, he was for twenty years an editor of major reference books on contemporary world writing and on world film directors for the H. W. Wilson Company of New York. Wakeman co-founded and for twelve years co-edited a British poetry magazine, *The Rialto,* until in 1996 his wife, Hilary, became Rector of a Church of Ireland parish in West Cork. The Wakemans moved to Ireland that year, and in 1999 founded *THE SHOP: a MAGAZINE OF POETRY,* which they still co-edit. John Wakeman's own poems have appeared in many journals and anthologies and in two collections, *A Room for Doubt* and *A Sea Family.* He has also published essays, reviews, feature articles, and prize-winning short stories, and has written for radio in the United States, Britain, and Ireland.

Derek Walcott was born in Saint Lucia, the West Indies, in 1930. He received his degree from the University of the West Indies, and in 1957 was awarded a fellowship by the Rockefeller Foundation to study the American theater. He founded the Trinidad Theater Workshop and his play *Dream on Monkey Mountain* won the Obie Award for distinguished foreign play of 1971. He also received the 1992 Nobel Prize in Literature, a MacArthur Foundation "genius" award, a Royal Society of Literature Award, and, in 1988, the Queen's Medal for Poetry. Some of Walcott's poetry collections include *Tiepolo's Hound, The Bounty, Omeros, The Arkansas Testament, The Fortunate Traveller, The Star-Apple Kingdom, Sea Grapes, The Gulf, The Castaway,* and *In a Green Night.* He is also the writer of essays, *What the Twilight Says,* and some of his plays include *The Odyssey: A Stage Version, The Isle Is Full of Noises,* and *Remembrance and Pantomime.* Derek Walcott lives in St. Lucia and teaches creative writing at Boston University in the fall.

Hutch Waters is the author of *Africa in Brooklyn.*

Michael Waters is Professor of English at Salisbury State University on the Eastern Shore of Maryland, and teaches in the New England College MFA Program in Poetry. The recipient of a Fellowship in Creative Writing from the National Endowment for the Arts, Individual Artist Awards from the Maryland State Arts Council, and three Pushcart Prizes, he is the author of eight poetry collections, including *Darling Vulgarity.*

Jerry Wemple was born in Dunmore, Pennsylvania, in 1960. He received his B.A. from Vermont College and his M.F.A. from the University of Massachusetts, Amherst. He served in the U.S. Navy from 1982 to 1988 and was a newspaper reporter in Massachusetts. He co-founded and runs The Big Dog Reading Series. His poetry collection is entitled *You Can See It from Here.* Wemple lives in Bloomsburg, Pennsylvania, and teaches creative writing at Bloomsburg University.

Walt Whitman (1819–1892) was born into a family of nine children, and spent his childhood in Brooklyn and Long Island. Among his many careers were printer, schoolteacher, journalist for the Brooklyn *Daily Eagle* and *The Long Islander* (which he founded), nurse and selfless companion for the wounded during the Civil War, and clerk for the Department of the Interior. His lifelong singular pursuit, however, was the composition, publication, and ongoing revision of the editions of his groundbreaking *Leaves of Grass,* releasing a self-published first edition in 1855, and following it with refinements in 1856 and 1882. Following the last publication, he settled in a home in Camden, New Jersey, where he worked on his final book of poems, *Good-Bye, My Fancy,* and spent his last years.

Anne Pierson Wiese grew up in Brooklyn and lived there until very recently, when she was obliged to find cheaper lodging in Manhattan. Her first collection of poems, *Floating City,* won the 2006 Walt Whitman Award. She was also a winner of the 2004 "Discovery"/*The Nation* poetry prize. Her poems have appeared or are forthcoming in *The Nation, Quarterly West, Prairie Schooner, West Branch, The Alaska Quarterly Review, Porcupine, The Saint Ann's Review, The South Carolina Review,* and *Rattapallax,* among others.

C. K. Williams was born in Newark, New Jersey, in 1936. He is the author of numerous books of poetry, including *The Singing,* winner of the 2003 National Book Award; *Repair,* which won the 2000 Pulitzer Prize; *The Vigil; A Dream of Mind; Flesh and Blood,* which won the National Book Critics Circle Award; *Tar; With Ignorance; I Am the Bitter Name;* and *Lies.* Along with his prose memoir, *Misgivings,* and essay collection, *Poetry and Consciousness,* Williams has also published five works of translation, including works by Sophocles and Euripides. Williams teaches in the creative writing program at Princeton University and lives part of each year in Paris.

Jonah Winter is the author of *Maine* and *Amnesia.* His poems have appeared in recent issues of *The Literary Review, Boston Review, Ploughshares,* and *Ducky.* He recently made his operatic debut with the Metropolitan Opera.

acknowledgments

Agha Shahid Ali, "Bones" from *Call Me Ishmael Tonight: A Book of Ghazals* by Agha Shahid Ali. Copyright © 2003 by Agha Shahid Ali Literary Trust. Used by permission of W. W. Norton & Company, Inc.

Karen Alkaly-Gut, "Brooklyn" from *So Far, So Good* by Karen Alkaly-Gut, published by Sivan Press in Tel Aviv. Copyright _ 2004. Used by permission of the author.

Nuar Alsadir, "Walking Through Prospect Park with Susan." Copyright © by Nuar Alsadir. Used by permission of the author.

Anonymous, "The Legend of Coney Island, Part 1" from the collection *The History of Coney Island from Its First Discovery in 4,11,44, Down to the Last Night, In Rhyme,* published by Morrison, Richardson & Co. in New York.

John A. Armstrong, "A Ditty of Greenpoint" from *Harvest: A Melange Relating to Brooklyn City in Particular and the World in General* by John A. Armstrong, published in Brooklyn in 1872.

L. S. Asekoff, "Widows of Gravesend" previously appeared in the *Brooklyn Review* (# 19, 2002). Copyright © 2002 by L. S. Asekoff. Used by permission of the author.

Andrea Baker, "West Street." The poem first appeared in *3rd Bed.* Copyright © 2007 by Andrea Baker. Reprinted by permission of the author.

Amiri Baraka, "The Bridge" from *Preface to a Twenty Volume Suicide Note.* Copyright © 1961 by Amiri Baraka. Reprinted by permission of the author.

Stanley H. Barkan, "On the Milkboxes" from *The Patterson Literary Review '89,* edited by Maria Mazziotti Gillan. Copyright © 1989 by Stanley H. Barkan. Reprinted by permission of the author.

Ed Barrett, "The Living End" from *Sheepshead Bay* by Ed Barrett. Copyright © 2001 by Ed Barrett. Reprinted by permission of the author.

Melissa Beattie-Moss, "Cancer Phobia." Copyright © 2007 by Melissa Beattie-Moss. Used by permission of the author.

Joshua Beckman, excerpt from "About the Days" from *Something I Expected To Be Different* (Verse Press 2001) by Joshua Beckman. Copyright © 2001 by Joshua Beckman. Reprinted by permission of Verse Press / Wave Books.

Ted Berrigan, "Personal Poem #9" from *The Collected Poems* by Ted Berrigan. Edited by Alice Notley. Copyright © NYP Alice Notley. Reprinted by permission of The University of California Press.

Elizabeth Bishop. "Invitation to Miss Marianne Moore" from *The Complete Poems:1927–1979* by Elizabeth Bishop. Copyright © 1979, 1983 by Alice Helen Methfessel. Reprinted by permission of Farrar, Straus and Giroux, LLC.

Menke Katz, "Tempest in Borough Park" from *A Chair for Elijah* by Menke Katz. Copyright © 1985 by Menke Katz. Reprinted by permission of The Smith.

Diane Kendig, "Flatbush 1980: A State of the Carribean in Brooklyn." Copyright © 1987 by Diane Kendig. Reprinted by permission of the author.

Maurice Kenny, "Dead Morning in Brooklyn Heights" from *Only as Far as Brooklyn* by Maurice Kenny. Copyright © 1979 by Maurice Kenny. Used by permission of the author.

Galway Kinnell, "Fire in Luna Park," from *The Past* by Galway Kinnell. Copyright © 1985 by Galway Kinnell. Reprinted by permission of Houghton Mifflin Company. All rights reserved.

Noelle Kocot, "Brooklyn Sestina: June, 1975" from *4* by Noelle Kocot. Copyright © 2001 by Noelle Kocot. Reprinted by permission of Four Way Books.

Anthony Lacavaro, "The Old Italian Neighborhood." Copyright © 2007 by Anthony Lacavaro. Used by permission of the author.

Katherine Lederer, "In Brooklyn" from *Winter Sex* by Katy Lederer. Copyright © 2002 by Katherine Lederer. Reprinted by permission of Verse Press/ Wave Books.

Rika Lesser, "536 Saratoga Avenue" from *Growing Back: Poems 1972–92* by Rika Lesser. Copyright © 1997 by Rika Lesser. Reprinted by permission of The University of South Carolina Press.

Donald Lev, "Enemies Over Time" and "Over Brighton" from *Enemies Over Time* by Donald Lev. Copyright © 2000 by Donald Lev. Reprinted by permission of the author.

Phillis Levin, "The Brooklyn Botanic Garden" from *Temples and Fields* by Phillis Levin. Copyright © 1988 by Phillis Levin. Reprinted by permission of The University of Georgia Press.

Philip Levine, "The Unknowable" from *The Mercy: Poems* by Philip Levine. Copyright © 1999 by Philip Levine. Used by permission of Alfred A. Knopf, a division of Random House, Inc.

Mani Leyb, "I Am . . ." Translated by John Hollander, from *The Penguin Book of Modern Yiddish Verse* by Irving Howe, Ruth R. Wisse, and Khone Shmeruk. Copyright © 1987 by Irving Howe, Ruth Wisse, and Khone Shmeruk. Used by permission of Viking Penguin, a division of The Penguin Group (USA) Inc.

Matthew Lippman, "Swell of Flame." Copyright © 2007 by Matthew Lippman. Used by permission of the author.

Timothy Liu, "The Brooklyn Botanic Garden" previously appeared in *Urban Nature: Poems about Wildlife in the City,* edited by Laure-Anne Bosselaar, Milkweed Editions, 2000. Copyright © 2000 by Timothy Liu. Reprinted by permission of the author.

Federico García Lorca. "Sleepless City" from *Poet in New York* by Federico García Lorca. Translation copyright © 1988 by The Estate of Federico García Lorca, and Greg Simon and Steven F. White. Reprinted by permission of Farrar, Straus, and Giroux, LLC, and The Penguin Group (UK).

Audre Lorde, "Cables to Rage Or I've Been Talking on This Street Corner a Hell of a Long Time" from *New York Head Shop and Museum.* Copyright © 1997 The Estate of Audre Lorde. Reprinted by permission of the Charlotte Sheedy Literary Agency, Inc.

Robert Lowell, "In the Forties" from *Collected Poems* by Robert Lowell. Copyright © 2003 by Harriet Lowell and Sheridan Lowell. Reprinted by permission of Farrar, Straus and Giroux, LLC.

David Margolis, "Life Is Not Complicated and Hard, Life Is Simple and Hard." Copyright © 2007 by Judith Margolis. Used by permission of the author.

about the editors

Julia Spicher Kasdorf has lived in the Brooklyn neighborhoods of Fort Greene, Kensington, and Carroll Gardens. She has published two collections of poetry, *Eve's Striptease* and *Sleeping Preacher;* a collection of essays, *The Body and the Book: Writing from a Mennonite Life;* and a biography, *Fixing Tradition: Joseph W. Yoder, Amish American.* An associate professor of English and women's studies at the Pennsylvania State University, she lives in Bellefonte, Pennsylvania.

Michael Tyrell lives in Greenpoint, Brooklyn, where he was born. He is a Phi Beta Kappa graduate of New York University and received his MFA at the Iowa Writers' Workshop, where he was awarded a Teaching-Writing Fellowship. His poems have been published in many magazines, including *Agni, The Canary, Columbia, Dragonfire, The New England Review, The Paris Review, Ploughshares*, and *The Yale Review.* He was awarded scholarships from the Bread Loaf Writers' Conference and the James Merrill Writer in Residence program. His work has been cited in more than a dozen competitions, including the Walt Whitman Award and the Yale Series of Younger Poets. He is also a prose writer, and an actor who has studied at the Atlantic and Looking Glass theatre companies. A former editorial assistant at the *New Yorker* and awards director at The Academy of American Poets, Tyrell has taught writing at Hunter College, New York University, and Pace University.